What the Lotus Said

What the Lotus Said

A Journey to Tibet and Back

Eric Swanson

St. Martin's Press ❧ New York

www.stmartins.com

Library of Congress Cataloging-in-Publication Data
Swanson, Eric.
    What the lotus said : a journey to Tibet and back / Eric Swanson.
      p. cm.
    ISBN 0-312-26693-6
    1. Swanson, Eric—Journeys—China—Tibet.   2. Tibet (China)—
Description and travel.   I. Title.

DS786 .S92 2002
951'.50459—dc21

                                                              2001048991

First Edition: April 2002

10   9   8   7   6   5   4   3   2   1

For my sister, Noreen Byrne, who asked me recently when I was going to dedicate a book to her

CONTENTS

ACKNOWLEDGMENTS

Tibetan Buddhists speak of life as a stream of being, a constantly evolving web of causes and conditions appearing in unique form at any given moment. I would like to take this opportunity to express my gratitude to certain individuals who have influenced the force and direction of the odd stream that has manifested as this book. Chief among those whose kindness can never be repaid are my Root Lama and the many great masters of the Tibetan Buddhist tradition who have taught me how to see and what to look for. For their endless tolerance, I must also thank the monks and nuns upstate, as well as all the people who shared their lives with me in Tibet. I thank my companions on the journey for the relief and laughter they afforded me; my agent, Emma Sweeney, for her undying support; Laura Bucko, for her constant sweetness; Andrew Miller, for his taste and judgment; Nichole Argyres and Diane Higgins for firmly, gently shepherding this manuscript to completion; Beth Crehan, Cecilia Zalak, Michelle Roguso, Jen Meyer, Dorothy Engelhardt, Linda Wegrzyn, and Edie Passno for cheering me on; and Bob Dombroski for putting up with me as long as he did.

It may be that gulfs will wash us down;
It may be we shall touch the Happy Isles...

—Alfred, Lord Tennyson, "Ulysses"

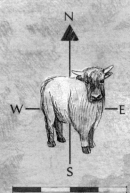

QINGHAI
PROVINCE

N

W——E

S

Approx. 100
statute miles

Mekong River

Lhasa
(Xra-sa)

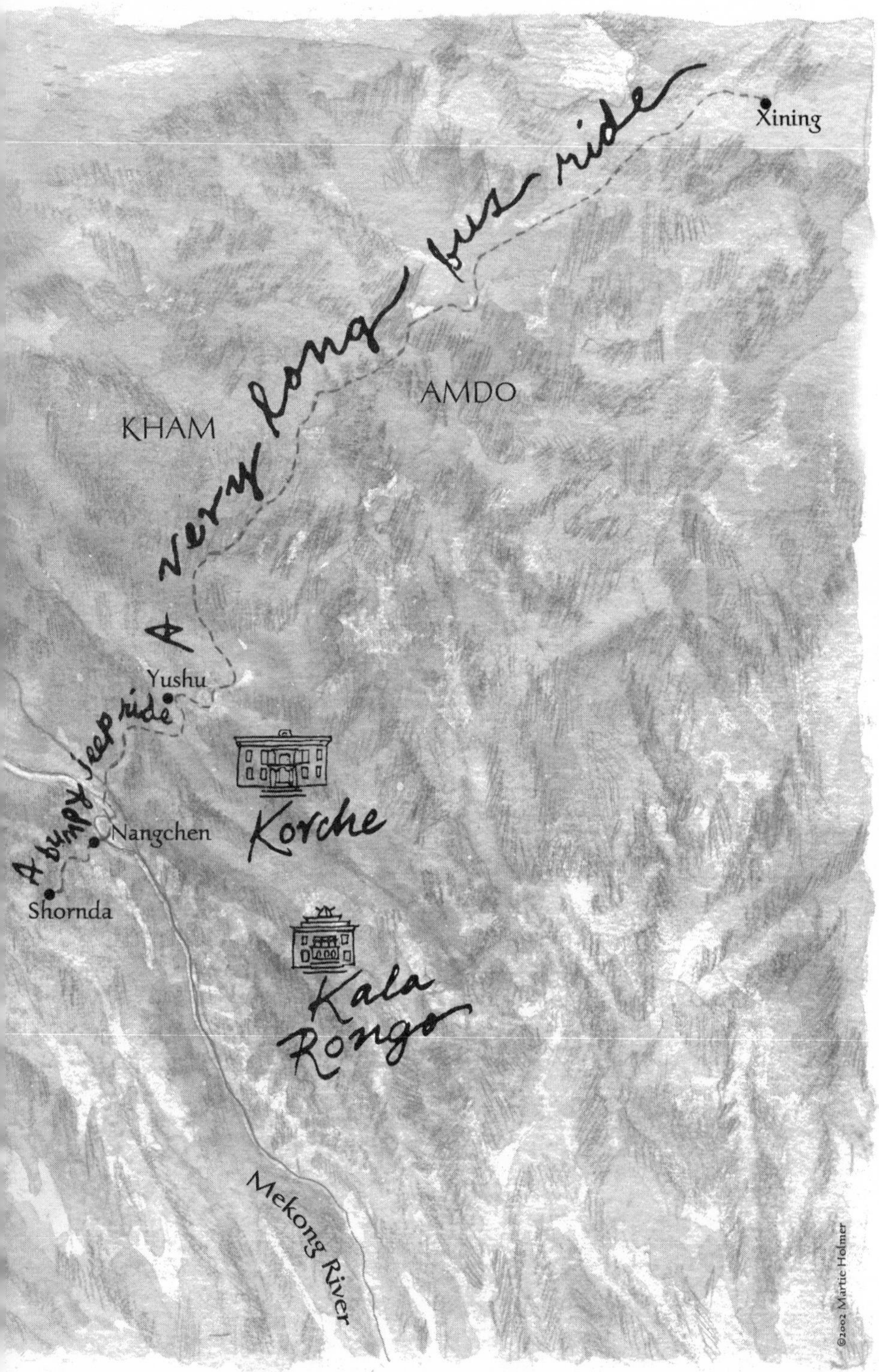

Xining

AMDO

KHAM

A very long bus ride

Yushu

A bumpy jeep ride

Korche

Nangchen

Shornda

Kala Rongo

Mekong River

©2002 Martie Holmer

Book of the Dead

ONE

Redundant to say that the bus has stopped in the middle of nowhere. East Tibet more or less defines the term: a bleak, gargantuan plateau ringed by mountains, punctuated every hundred miles or so by a yak-skin tent, a herd of goats. It's the Moon, the South Pole, the Antipodes of legend. A landscape familiar through dreams, difficult to pinpoint but indelibly real. A likely enough place, in other words, for a bus to wait out the night.

It is night of course. It's also the third time the bus has stopped for a blown tire, caused in some small part by the weight of eighty people crammed onto a bus designed for fifty: Tibetans, Chinese, Mongolians, plus our group of four Americans. Those who'd bought tickets back in Yushu, the starting point of the trip, are lucky enough to spend the twenty-some-hour ride stretched out in a semiprone position, as a ticket earns a place on one of the bunks lining both sides of the bus. There are upper bunks and lower bunks, each about a foot and a half wide and five feet long. The thin foam mattresses smell of old sweat, dirt, and motor oil; and the blankets allotted each passenger are alive with fleas.

Still, we're better off than the people who've been picked up along the way, bribing the driver for a place in the aisle, where they suffer accidental pelting with sunflower seed husks, bits of corn, cigarette butts. They have to pass the rumbling, jostling hours squatting on cardboard boxes crammed with their worldly goods or hefty sacks of rice or—worse—burlap bags full of yak butter, the odor of which is acrid, like a long-buried cache of dirty socks.

Given the overcrowding and the fact that most of the passengers are accompanied by prodigious amounts of luggage, it's not surprising that the tires, already worn with age and use, would give up the ghost.

The back left tire is the first to blow. Fortunately, the disaster occurs quite close to one of the Muslim restaurants that periodically appear oasislike and without logistical connection to any town or village along our route. While the driver and his assistant labor at repairs, most of the passengers crowd into the restaurant—a dark, low-ceilinged place, where Mongolian women in long skirts, their dark, oval faces framed by heavy scarves, pass among the tables serving up bowls of hot spiced noodles and small, round loaves of pan-cooked bread. A wondrous meal chased down with lukewarm Pepsi.

After dinner, we shuffle somewhat reluctantly back onto the bus, and the driver steers us back onto the road north toward Xining, a city in northwest China, our antepenultimate destination. There is still the flight from Xining to Beijing, and from there the longer trip back to the States.

The second tire, the front right, blows about half an hour after we set out. Repairs take longer this time, or at least they seem to, without the distraction of a hot meal. Dusk falls swiftly as we wait: a gray-green mist slowly melting distant mountaintops.

All of a sudden, it's dark.

The third stop, a few hours after we're back on the road, is the longest by far. Few people bother this time to step out to see what's wrong or even to stretch their legs. It's too cold out, for one thing. Also, a collective apathy seems to have overtaken all the passengers, a more or less grudging acceptance of misfortune. The tinkering, clanking, and occasional shouts from outside continue for maybe half an hour before curiosity at last compels me to climb down from my bunk and out into the keen, frigid air of the Tibetan night.

Ten or twelve others have collected at the front of the bus. I can also see several people making their way back from various places along the side of the road. I don't necessarily feel the call of nature, but you can never tell how many hours might pass between misfortunes, so it's best to take advantage of these unchartered stops along the way. I walk about twenty yards across the lumpy, uneven tundra till I reach a reasonably secluded spot. The sound of peeing pierces the night's huge silence, along with an occasional groan or belch.

The sky forms a nearly perfect bowl curving toward the distant horizon; a dense, refulgent darkness pierced by icy stars. A dimension of night that might, with only a little greater effort of the senses, be touched or tasted. The sheer enormity of the shadowed landscape arouses sentimental notions of infinity and timelessness, danger-ous associations that I have begun to distrust, largely as a result of my stay in Tibet. Yet in spite of my efforts to remain clearheaded, as I head back toward the bus I can almost feel one of my feet sinking into the ground, just as though the tales of mystical experience that had moved me to come here were momentarily true: I'm stepping through matter, sliding vertically through time and space.

Actually, it's yak dung. The field is dotted with large,

round pats of it, indistinguishable in the dark from clumps of dried mud.

"Ever wonder," someone behind me asks, "what Martha Stewart might do with one of those?"

The voice belongs to Martha, a member of our small group of Americans visiting Tibet ostensibly to perform good works—though I'm willing to concede that we all have personal agendas, uniquely inarticulable motivations. Martha is a Bard student, tall, red-haired, originally from Texas. Young. Younger than I am, which is the crucial distinction, one that has begun to include more and more people.

For a moment we stand together under the merciless stars, the baronial dark, pondering the uses of yak dung.

"Decorative centerpiece," I suggest. "Put a little house on it, some trees, fake snow."

"Trivets," Martha says.

"Coasters."

"Yak dung. It's a good thing."

We wander back toward the bus. The group at the front has grown into a haphazard line of men raptly watching the progress of the repairs. Some of the onlookers are dressed in old blue Mao suits or military uniforms, others wearing fedoras, ragged suit coats thrown over their shoulders, pants belted with rope. Young Tibetan men tend to dress like 1930s gangsters; or as migrant workers, types seen staring bleakly out of a John Ford film, complete with caps and dirty vests, lengths of rag twisted jauntily around their necks. They smoke constantly, holding their cigarettes at cocky angles between the thumb and the first two fingers. Most carry daggers on their hips.

The bus's headlights cut a yellow swath across the line of onlookers. Bravely illuminated against the enormous night, the ragged group of Tibetans, Mongolians, and Chinese is a WPA mural brought to sudden life. The effect owes as much to the outdated clothes and weary gravitas of the onlookers as to their absolute engagement in the project at hand. An absorption incompatible with irony or comment, the radiance of saints and simple men. It's hard to resist the urge to romanticize the scene, to attribute meaning where there may be none.

Just as Martha and I reach the road, the driver wriggles out from under the bus and barks out orders to his assistant. Gradually, the crowd breaks up, reassembling in smaller groups along the sides of the road. A middle-aged Chinese man detaches himself from the group and heads for the open field. As he passes I ask him, in halting and inchoate Chinese, if he knows what's going on. As far as I understand his reply, the front right tire has been damaged past all hope of repair. We simply have to wait until another bus comes by and hope they have an extra tire we might be able to use. When I ask him if he has any idea when that might be, he shrugs. "Maybe one hour," he replies, "maybe three."

I can't tell whether his response is vague or my grasp of Chinese grammar is too limited to allow comprehension of subtle connotations. I learned Chinese too quickly, a crash course in a small foreign language school on West Fifty-seventh Street that had advertised in the *Village Voice*. I can understand his next remark more easily because it sounds like something out of one of my language study guides.

"Surely," he says, "it will be no more than a day."

As I struggle to absorb this new bit of information—reviewing the impact of a long delay on our itinerary—he asks me if I'm French. To which I reply that no, I'm American. He nods vigorously and tells me he has a cousin in America. Or maybe a nephew. I'm not sure of the word he's used.

He opens his suit coat to show me the T-shirt he's wearing. It's an attempt at an American jersey, an article commonly worn by children and teenagers in Tibet, and usually emblazoned with ersatz English phrases like FASHION TO YOU! or HAPPY CHRISTIAN!

The Chinese man's shirt says NOT KANSAS!

I smile and nod and tell him it's very nice. At least I hope that's what I told him. Given the inaccuracy of my pronunciation, I may have said it was "*Very four*" or "*Very death.*"

He seems pleased enough with my response though. We stand beaming and nodding for a long moment, then he excuses himself and resumes his journey out to the field.

Martha has already settled back in her bunk when I

return to the bus; but she's still awake, so I tell her what I've learned about the tire. The other two members of our party have taken advantage of the lengthy pause to attempt sleep. It seems pointless to wake them just to say we're not going anywhere, so I simply hoist myself up into my bunk to wait out the night.

Several minutes later my Chinese friend climbs aboard and sidles down the narrow aisle toward his own bunk. He stops when he sees me and very slowly and precisely says, in English, "Good night." Then he continues down the aisle.

A cloud of cigarette smoke sails forward out of the darkness from the back of the bus, and someone starts rustling in a paper bag of nuts or seeds. Someone a few rows behind me switches on a cassette player; but after a few muttered complaints, it's switched off.

I turn toward the window, watching a small group of men still standing outside. Laughter punctuates their conversation, a bottle passes between hands, cigarettes are lit. The smokers bend toward one another, cupping hand to hand to protect matches against the wind. I could envy their camaraderie, the sense of ordinariness they exude, as if their place in the world were not a hazard or a mystery.

"The trip will change you," a Canadian nun had said somewhat wistfully before I left for Tibet. I knew she'd wanted to come with us, but too many obstacles prevented her. So I promised to bring back some water from a river blessed by Tibet's patron saint: an eighth-century adept named Padmasambhava.

I've made good on my promise. There's a jar of water in my suitcase, wrapped first in a pair of dirty jeans and then again in a towel. Getting the water took some effort, and I don't want the jar to break. I am concerned, though, because the water is filled with parasites. I wonder if the Canadian nun intends to drink it or just keep the jar on her personal altar. I wonder if boiling the water to kill the parasites will somehow eliminate the saint's blessing, the way cooking destroys vitamins. I wonder if the parasites are blessed by virtue of living in water once stepped in by a holy man.

I feel a similar ambivalence toward the other things I'm carrying out of Tibet, lodged somewhere in my entrails, small and alien, stirring up trouble. I wonder what virtues they possess, what dangers they may pose.

As I settle down to try and sleep, I wonder if another bus will actually come by within a day, and if so, whether we'll make our flight from Xining to Beijing in time to get our flight back to the States.

I hope so.

I'm tired of Not-Kansas.

I want to go home.

TWO

An embarrassing fact: I was thirty-six years old before I found out Tibet was a real place. Before then I'd conflated the actual country with the fictional paradise of *Lost Horizon,* Shangri-la. When people ask how I ended up in Tibet, I find myself fumbling for an answer because I had no deep yearning to go; the invitation came fairly suddenly, and I accepted without much hesitation. I would have done the same if I'd been asked to visit Mars or the Moon: for the sake of adventure, the appeal of the unknown—both echoes of a childhood infatuation with the idea of space travel that had spontaneously bloomed when I was ten.

I'd spent a lot of afternoons in the basement of our house building models of the *Apollo, Mercury,* and *Gemini* spacecraft, carefully scraping dried excess glue from surfaces, making sure the doors and escape hatches functioned properly; I belonged to a book club for junior space explorers; I knew obscure technical specifications of the lunar module. I was dead set on becoming an astronaut until one of my older brothers informed me that astronauts couldn't wear glasses: An astronaut, he explained, wouldn't be able to see anything if his glasses broke during a crash landing. For me it was a defining disappointment; my brother doesn't remember the exchange.

My mother, meanwhile, had begun taking yoga classes, an attempt to ease the stress thought to underlie an elaborate regimen of involuntary vocal tics and twitches that would eventually be diagnosed as Tourette syndrome. She practiced meditation in our living room, her face cemented in an expression of determined tranquility. Books on Eastern metaphysics began turning up around the house, stuffed between sofa cushions, tucked between volumes I and II of *Mastering the Art of French Cooking*. Line drawings of physical contortions competed with Ayurvedic remedies requiring almond oil or turmeric, various proofs of reincarnation, lessons in cleansing the intestines by inserting a long stip of cloth through the nose and pulling it out through the anus. What caught my attention were the oblique references to astral projection, soul travel to other worlds. Passing through time as easily as water.

I started haunting the shelves of what used to be

known as the occult section of the local Waldenbooks in search of more specific instruction. Methodologies. Between the ages of twelve and seventeen, I acquired a small but impressive library of arcane publications that included meditation manuals and astrological guides, the prophecies of Edgar Cayce, compendiums of black magic, histories of the Masons, and pamphlets from the Society of Rosicrucians. I spent hours in my bedroom staring at candle flames and focusing my mind on dots drawn on the wall, muttering over bowls of clear water, breathing in sandalwood incense.

Such effort.

In college, there were drugs; there was alcohol. Material mechanisms of leaving the body that soon became nonviable. I went to acting school, became an actor—in plays, small films—which accomplished a projection of sorts, not quite out of body, but at least toward a field of being more imaginative, less ordinary. Then I became I writer.

Along the way I developed an addiction to spiritual seeking, trying various disciplines such as Zen, Kashmir Shaivism, Bioenergetics. Self-Realization. EST. Scientology. A list like Homer's catalogue of ships. I collected crystals and chanted special syllables to open my chakras. During a visit to Berkeley, I had my aura cleaned. I was rebirthed.

In the process I uncovered some interesting asides: compulsions of varying strengths and consequence, delicately armed strategies of self-sabotage, memories and fabrications spontaneously erected to conceal the more egregious blank spots. For example, I had convinced myself that my interest in space had originated with Neil Armstrong stepping onto the surface of the Moon. I can recall without hesitation leaning against the door of our den, my father supine on the couch, my little brother huddled behind his giant knees. July 20, 1969. The bluish flickering of the TV screen.

I was in the middle of having my polarity adjusted when I realized that this story, which I'd trotted out on a number of where-were-you-when social occasions, wasn't strictly true. Yes, I'd watched Neil Armstrong. But a full month before the *Eagle* landed in the Sea of Tranquility, my uncle collapsed while playing golf, and died twenty-four hours later.

The wake lasted two days; the funeral, a third. Massed flowers. A grieving mob of relatives and friends. The casket was open, and the man, my uncle, displayed like packaged meat: a lurid bit of pageantry euphemistically referred to as a *viewing*. Wherein may be read a call, perhaps, to see.

I saw myself, mostly, the embarrassment I felt over not being sad enough, and the fear that someone would find out. Sometimes I looked up, catching the smell of lilies mingling with perfume, the restrained murmur of small groups that formed in corners. My mother led me twice each day to the coffin and squeezed my hand until I kissed my uncle's dead cheek.

Once, I got caught between the coffin and a stand of flowers, in a clumsy dance with a woman on her way up to view the corpse as I was heading back. She stopped, inquired whose son I was, where I fit in the lineup of siblings and cousins. I ran out of answers when I noticed that she had no eyebrows. Whatever she'd been born with had been plucked out or lost, and above each eye she'd drawn a perfect arc in brown, thick pencil. She asked me what grade I was in, what I wanted to be when I grew up.

I thought of John Glenn, drifting in a space capsule, mercifully alone, above, and replied that I was going to be an astronaut.

It was in the winter of 1995 that, on the advice of a friend, I started phoning various Tibetan Buddhist centers in New York City. There were quite a lot of them. Most of the time I spoke to answering machines obediently leaving my name and number, the best times to be reached. I'd almost reached the bottom of the list by the time I spoke to an actual person, a woman who told me that the lama connected with that particular center was, in fact, giving an empowerment that afternoon. I had to ask what a lama was.

"*Lama* is the Tibetan word for guru," she explained. "A meditation master."

I also had to ask what an empowerment was; and after

a fractional hesitation, she replied that it was a kind of blessing. I supposed it wouldn't hurt to try.

Half an hour later, I found myself in Chelsea, pressing a buzzer at the entrance to a dilapidated loft building. Minutes passed. Finally a woman with dark hair came out to the fire escape five stories above and threw down a key, which was wrapped in a sock. She shouted down instructions, telling me to use the key to open the front door, then take the stairs to the fifth floor. After some trouble with the door, I eventually gained entry and made my way up a perilous set of stairs: dark and narrow, thick with dust, every few steps a weak board. At the fifth-floor landing, a massive red door stood open. The same woman who had thrown down the key now sat behind a tray table wedged in the doorway of a cramped office across from the door. Dark hair, large glasses. She welcomed me, smiling, and asked how I was doing. I replied that I was a little out of breath after the stairs.

She nodded. "Everybody says that at first. Are you here for the empowerment?"

"Yes. I called half an hour ago. Was it you I spoke to?"

"I don't think so. Have you taken refuge?"

To my left was a sort of waiting room, most of which was occupied by a table. The walls were brick, painted yellow. There was a dirty blue carpet on the floor. About twenty people stood or sat in the waiting room, sipping herbal tea from Styrofoam cups, murmuring, trading nervous, cheery smiles: a pale, quietly eccentric group in their handwoven sweaters, frizzy hair, oversized jewelry. I suddenly thought of the last scene of *Rosemary's Baby*.

"What do you mean by 'refuge'?" I asked.

The woman smiled broadly as if I'd paid her an especially warm compliment.

"You could think of it as an extra blessing," she said. "Not absolutely necessary for this empowerment, but it'll give it a little more—"

She searched.

"Oomph," I suggested.

"Exactly. Oomph."

I asked if refuge would cost more, something of a concern as I had only forty dollars in my wallet. She assured me it wouldn't, so I paid her and she handed me a receipt.

"Let me go arrange things with Lama," she said, standing and squeezing around the tray table. She disappeared behind a thin curtain strung across the hallway on my right.

I stepped into the waiting area and sat down next to a short, wiry, bald man with bulging, blue eyes. We traded quick, bland smiles. Waiting room etiquette.

The table in the middle of the room was spread with long strips of sheer white cloth. Before I could ask what they were used for, everybody turned toward the narrow hallway where the woman who had greeted me at the door had disappeared. Those who were sitting stood.

Everyone held their hands palms together in front of their chests and bowed their heads slightly. Not to be rude, I followed suit.

Moments later, a small, barefoot man in maroon robes walked into the room. He was about five and a half feet tall and round in a way that didn't seem disproportionate with his height. A bit of gray stubble covered his head. He smiled very warmly and waved as he passed among us, chuckling and murmuring, "Hello, hello."

Following close behind him was a young American woman with a shaved head. She also wore maroon robes. Together they entered a room to the left of the waiting area. A blonde woman pulled a pair of gold silk curtains across the entrance and ducked behind them herself. People resumed their seats, gathered the threads of their conversations.

"That's Lama," the short man sitting next to me confided, winking.

"And who was that with him?" I asked.

He said a name that I couldn't quite make out. It sounded like Sambo. Later I would learn that her name was Zangmo, a Tibetan name given at her ordination. She was, the man sitting next to me explained, Lama's translator.

A gravelly chanting came from behind the gold curtain, accompanied by the rhythmic clanging of a bell and occasional rapid bursts of clattering. The man next to me leaned close and, in a bright stage whisper, informed me that Lama was preparing the shrine room for the empowerment. I nodded and sat with my eyes closed, trying to still my mind by breathing deeply while visualizing white light seeping into my body through the crown of my head, a technique I'd learned from the slightly oily, middle-aged man who had cleaned my aura in Berkeley.

After five minutes the blonde woman stepped through the curtains into the waiting room to ask who was waiting to take refuge. I was the only one to raise a hand. A desperate and unpleasant moment. Had I known, I almost certainly would have kept still. I would have pretended to be an old hand at refuge.

I stepped gamely toward the curtained room though. The blonde woman asked me to please take off my shoes—politely, almost embarrassed, a tone reserved for funeral homes and hospital waiting rooms. I removed my shoes and someone offered to put them by the coat rack near the front door. Then I stepped through the gold curtains.

The floor of the shrine room was covered with red industrial carpeting. The walls were yellow with glossy red trim around each of the three windows. Long strips of yellow and orange silk had been hung along the ceiling to hide the pipes that ran around the tops of the walls. Round maroon pillows had been lined up neatly in rows along the floor. Directly in front of me stood two tall thrones covered in silk cloths of various colors and embroidered with dragons, wheels, diamond shapes, and stylized flowers. Lama wasn't sitting on either throne but instead on a cushioned platform very low to the floor. His translator sat on the floor next to him.

Against the wall to my right stood an altar consisting of several tiers covered with embroidered silks. Small brass bowls full of water occupied the lower shelves, interspersed with small candles burning in metal holders shaped like tiny grails. The remaining space was occupied by statues of the Buddha, variously sized, some painted, others plain. There were photographs as well; men I didn't recognize. Teachers, I thought. Holy men.

I plopped awkwardly on the floor in front of the lama. He looked at me somewhat startled and, I thought, a bit sternly before starting to speak in a language I assumed was Tibetan: a palatal, incantatory music, periodically surprised by a drawn-out vowel. The translator wrote on a pad; and after the lama stopped, she began to read aloud from her notes.

"Please begin by giving rise to the attitude of perfect Bodhicitta," she began, "which is the thought that all sentient beings, who have been your mothers and whose numbers fill the whole expanse of space, must by all means be brought to the level of completely perfect Buddhahood."

She had a soft voice, carefully neutral. The tips of her ears flushed as she spoke.

"And think," she continued, "that in order to bring

this about, you will listen to and put into practice the teachings of the profound Mahayana Dharma."

I had no idea what she was talking about.

Buddhism is a complex religion, a nexus of philosophical speculation, practice, and revelation. The historical Buddha, Siddhartha Gautama, is said to have abandoned his place among the Indian ruling class after three secret trips outside his father's palace revealed to him the grim realities of life: old age, sickness, and finally, death. A sheltered prince confronted by a corpse. One thinks of Hamlet. The Buddha responded, not through madness but self-mortification, seeking to crush attachment to the mortal coil by torturing his flesh; but after years of trying, he found himself no closer to an answer to the problem of suffering. So he ate. He clothed himself. He sat in the shade of a tall *Ficus religiosa*, quieting his mind with meditative techniques he had learned early in his ascetic training.

And as he grew still, his mind touched something raw below the threshold of awareness: *duhkha* it's called in Sanskrit, a strong but subtle current of unease. The feeling may not have been new to him; sooner or later, most meditators collide against some form of discomfort— muscle cramps, emotional fluctuations, restless mental chatter. What the Buddha brought to the experience, the pearl wrested from his prior failures, was a willingness to abide with his unease. To watch, to listen, to learn.

Duhkha observed loses its solidity, reveals itself as an

instantaneous series of mental fabrications, like waves ruffling surface of a lake. The Buddha watched them come and go, and gradually discerned their source: *trishna*, thirst, a fundamental dissatisfaction with the way things are, and a restless search for something better, greater, more gratifying, just around the corner. We suffer because we thirst; we thirst because we suffer. This is the law of karma: not a cosmic punishment for bad decisions, or a reward for deeds well done, but a simple equation of cause and effect. Karma is a habit of perception that we accept as truth.

Understanding the transparent nature of *duhkha* may have prepared the Buddha for the next step: observing his perceptions without engaging them. This would require courage. We may chafe at our beliefs, but they're at least familiar. Who are we if we're not who we think we are? The answer can occur only in the negative. Not that. Not that. Not that. Until you arrive at an experience of being without reference or limit. Emptiness, the Buddha called this state: *shunyata*. Not a blank, not a void, but a refulgence beyond the mind's ability to define by name.

When the Buddha emerged from his meditative state, he realized that any attempt to communicate his discovery to other people would be futile. But Brahma, the Creator God, appeared to him and begged him to change his mind: "For the sake of those with only a few grains of dust in their eyes."

So he tried; he taught; crisscrossing India until his death in the first part of the fifth century B.C.E. During the fifteen hundred years after his death, as sects and schisms developed among the inheritors of his teaching, as Buddhists competed for patronage with other religious groups and popular cults, and as the Dharma spread to other lands across Central and eastern Asia, a variety of elaborations emerged and were eventually organized into a system of three vehicles, known in Sanskrit as *yana*.

The Hinayana, or narrow vehicle, focuses on individual liberation—the cessation of personal suffering in all its manifestations—through discipline and meditation. The Mahayana, or great vehicle, extends the field of liberation to include all beings endowed with consciousness. The Vajrayana, or indestructible vehicle, requires a creative leap, an existential recognition of the source of all experience, all beings, in the inherently pure mind of enlightenment. Sacred texts describe this mind as luminous, omnipresent, omniscient awareness, uncreated and therefore indestructible. The words, it's taught, are only signposts. The mind of enlightenment is beyond description, beyond categories of appearance and nonappearance, existence and nonexistence.

These distinctions would resolve themselves only gradually, through exposure, through repetition. Even so, my understanding of the differences remained for a long time largely conceptual. To make the jump from philosophy to fact, I would have to learn the language. I would have to meditate. I would have to study with survivors of the Tibetan diaspora, aged men and exiles carrying the teachings West. I would have to visit Tibet.

After the refuge ceremony, after the empowerment, I was ushered into a small room at the opposite end of the loft from the shrine room. The lama sat on a low cot, while Zangmo, his translator, sat cross-legged a few feet away on the floor. It was warm in the room; the radiator banged and whistled, first sign of winter in New York.

I had purchased a string of sandalwood prayer beads in the center's small bookstore; and on the advice of the woman who'd sold them to me, I asked the lama to bless them. He ran the beads through his fingers several times, blew on them, and handed them back to me. Through Zangmo, he asked if I had any questions.

I had dozens, of course; but the accumulated detritus of several years of spiritual shopping summed up succinctly was the first that rolled out of my mouth.

"What am I supposed to get out of this?"

I believe Zangmo gasped.

The lama raised his eyebrows and tilted his head one way and then the other, considering me a long moment over the rim of his teacup. One of the few instances I can recall being studied, measured, with complete candor.

"Very simple," he replied in English. "A way to die."

THREE

Legends say that *The Tibetan Book of the Dead* lay buried for a thousand years before it was found in the hills of Central Tibet. The man who found the text, furthermore, was said to be an incarnation of one of the original disciples of the saint who composed it: an Afghani adept, trained in India, where he was given the name Padmasambhava, the Lotus-Born.

The text was meant to be whispered in the ear of a person recently deceased. Its grim imagery abounds in blood-drinking monsters, women with wolves' heads, intense heat, piercing cold. Comfort has no place in the state between death and rebirth.

Padmasabhava's aim was not to comfort but to illumine. At every turn the deceased is urged to look closely and feel deeply, to recognize the nightmare unfolding around him as a projection of his own mind. But because each encounter is an exercise in terror, the opportunity to see the calm truth behind appearances is usually lost. Disembodied, overcome by anxiety, the mind of the deceased looks so desperately for shelter that a crack in a rock appears a welcome sight; even hell seems preferable to endless wandering.

Though I wonder. It seems to me there might be places more hopeless and terrifying than a nightmare realm of ceaseless wandering.

Beijing airport, for example. It's not the size that terrifies; though the terminal is ludicrously unsuited to the volume of travelers passing through China now. It's an old building, veneered walls, beige linoleum, low ceilings—early sixties I would hazard. Scuffed, cracked, and slightly filthy. A utilitarian blandness gone to seed. It's hard to deny the claustrophobic pressure, the cramped customs lines, the massed swelling around the luggage tracks, the shouting and pushing.

More than the physical discomfort is the sense, once the border guard has examined my passport, snapped it shut, and officially approved my entrance into China, that the trip has shifted from the idea stage to the real. We are—undeniably, irreclaimably—here.

We includes myself, Lama, Zangmo, and Martha. Beijing is merely the first step on our way to Nangchen, a remote mountainous region in Kham, where Lama was born. Lama has gone back there every year since the

1980s, establishing schools, rebuilding monasteries, and bringing professional medical support to local farmers and nomads who would otherwise have nothing.

Each of us has our special function on this trip. Martha, for example, is a photography major at Bard College; her job will be to film and photograph key moments—clinics, classroom visits, special ceremonies. The footage and photographs will be transmogrified into fund-raising materials when we return to the States.

Zangmo is responsible for the logistical and financial aspects of the trip: tracking expenses, handling receipts, and overseeing the yearly accounting process at Lama's two monasteries. Also making sure that all our tickets and hotel arrangements are in order and that the appropriate documents are presented at government offices throughout our journey.

I have two jobs, the less conspicuous of which is to protect Lama: physically, if need be, but primarily just by looking tall, strong, and capable. I am, at least, tall; the rest would have to be inferred. Still, the need for even the admittedly illusory services of a bodyguard is real. Tibet is old. The memory of clan feuds, religious wars, invasions, and alliances haunts the soil and paints the mountains with a mourning feel of desolation. The last two kings of the Tibetan empire died by assassination. Hired armies—Mongol, Chinese—shored up the rule of their weak successors. Rival schools of sacred learning armed their monks and burned each other's institutions. A complex, bloody history unjustly served by the modern image of Tibetans as kindly Munchkins. There are thieves and murderers, now as then. Every household, every nomad camp, keeps dogs raised deliberately for viciousness. Old women carry daggers in their belts. It's the Wild West, Tibet. Open, enticing, and hazardous.

My other, more conspicuous job is to look after the luggage, of which there is a prodigious amount. At Kennedy airport the procession of baggage unloaded by the nuns and monks from Lama's New York monastery was close to inspiring: bulging suitcases tied with rope or held shut with elastic straps; boxes full of school supplies, gifts, sacred texts, liturgical objects; to say nothing of personal effects—the multiweather clothing, sleeping bags, dried food, protein bars, tea, candles, flashlights, cameras. Items selected and stowed to ensure a minimum of creature comfort. Toilet paper. Soap.

Unfortunately none of these personal, communal, and charitable effects have arrived in Beijing. At the luggage claims office—a plywood booth set with a sliding Plexiglas window—we learn from a stooped man with papery skin and thick glasses that our bags have missed the connection in Detroit. Probably. He can't say for sure, and sadly there is no one he can call. The Northwest Airlines office in Beijing has already closed for the day. He seems almost offended when I ask him when the next flight from Detroit is due to arrive.

"Yes, yes," he says shortly, pushing a form printed on thin, pale green paper through the window. He's already looking past us at the next couple in line, who are Chinese and presumably cultivated enough to know that his job is not to help or to answer questions but to pass out the form on which travelers can report their missing luggage.

A China Travel Service agent from our hotel meets us at the front of the airport. His name is Won, he tells us, adding that it should be easy to remember because it is so much like our English number one. He demonstrates by pointing up with his slim, macadamia-colored index finger. Won conducts us out of the terminal to the van we'd hired specially to convey our abundance of luggage. As we make our way across the parking lot, Won consoles us by saying that our bags will almost certainly arrive before we leave Beijing.

The air outside is filthy and hot, settling around us like a damp rag. By the time we reach the van, we've all begun to sweat. Our driver, who does not introduce himself, hurls the vehicle into the stampede of cars, taxis, and buses that clogs the expressway. Nonplused by the frequency of near-collisions that occur as we careen with the rest of the evening traffic toward Beijing, Won describes some of the activities he would be happy to arrange for us during out stay. He can offer us the best, the most comfortable tours of the Forbidden City, for example, at a much better rate than tour services not connected with our hotel. He can also arrange for a private van to the Great Wall, with a very knowledgeable driver and a very pleasant tour guide, also at a much better rate than we could find elsewhere. With a neat bow to Lama and Zangmo, he advises, in addition, that there is also a Lamaist temple in Beijing, very splendid and very beautiful, for which he can also arrange a tour, also at a very good price.

How layered, I wonder, is this exchange? *Lamaist* is a derogatory term used by European writers of the eighteenth and nineteenth centuries, who viewed Tibetan religious practice as a type of idolatry, a corrupt and purely nominal offshoot of Buddhism; a point of view shared, apparently, by the Chinese of the same period. My Chinese teacher back in New York had pointed out, somewhat sharply, that the Chinese term for Buddhism is *fo jiao*—teaching of the Buddha—whereas the word for Tibetan religion is *lama jiao*—teaching of the lama.

As he smiles and praises the beauty of the Lama temple, does Won know that he's insulted us? Or has the term *lama jiao*—and its English equivalent—settled so deeply and certainly into the language that the pejorative cast no longer obtains? Either way I find my trust in him eroding.

It takes nearly three-quarters of an hour to get to the hotel. Dusk descends as we pass along an endless stretch of brick wall, above which peek the tops of bleached yellow palm trees and anonymous stone buildings. And here's a surprise: Except for the palm trees, Beijing looks like Cleveland—the same sense of urban desperation. Weedy lots on either side of the roadway partially hide the bones of old buildings; in between sit rows of shabby brick apartment houses, ruined teeth spotted with black stains.

Eventually we arrive at an area overshadowed by several chunky skyscrapers, one of which turns out to be our hotel. A wasteland of muddy streets spreads out behind it, where barefoot men sell watermelons from wooden carts and ragged children skid, laughing and shrieking, around one-story hovels.

Our rooms are clean, the beds comfortable. Lama and I share one room, Zangmo and Martha another. In our room a recessed shelf next to the television holds a small refrigerator, cups, saucers, and a thermos full of hot water. It's customary, in China and in Tibet, to supply guests with fresh thermoses of hot water, morning and evening. There's no coffee; but I've been prepared for this and have spent several days before leaving New York doggedly transferring my allegiance to tea.

Zangmo and Martha join us after washing up in their room. For a while we exult in the air-conditioning, flipping through Chinese programs on the television as we gradually settle into postflight languor.

Martha, more industrious than we are, sets herself to study the pamphlets and folders that describe the hotel's amenities. "Oh, look," she says, "this hotel does not allow prostitutes."

Zangmo gets up from her chair. "It doesn't say that," she insists. She peers over Martha's shoulder.

"You're right, it does." Then she laughs. "No, see, they've spelled it wrong. The *p* is upside down. 'This hotel does not allow drostitutes.' Prostitutes are okay."

Apparently so, since at 2:30 that morning I find myself standing in the doorway trying to make a point to a uniformed hotel employee. Slightly behind him stands a marginally clothed young woman with short, black hair, the same woman, I assume, who has been calling our room throughout the night to ask we if want a late-night massage. She has shown herself adept at misunderstanding my repeated attempts to decline.

Just at this moment, she's staring haplessly down at the carpet and picking at her thumb with the nail of her index finger. I suspect she's realized she's made a mistake by shifting tactics, coming to the door, and trying to push her way inside when I answered. I wonder how the scene might have ended had the bellboy, or whoever he is, not walked down the hall at this particular moment.

I explain to him—half in Chinese, half in English— that I do not want a massage, I do not want phone calls, I want to sleep. He nods and smiles and repeats my words back to me until we're both sure we understand each other securely. Then he turns to the young woman and says something that sounds as if it may be harsh. She nods, barely lifting her head, and sighs through pursed lips. The bellboy turns back to me and smiles and says he wishes me good sleep.

He takes the young woman by the elbow and steers her down the hall toward the elevators. Something in the way her free arm trails behind at a wayward angle to her shoulder provokes a pang of sadness. I should be angry, having my sleep disturbed, my nerves balled up, the jangling telephone, the confrontation under bright fluorescent lights. Instead I feel like I've blundered; I've broken something. Ignorant, self-righteous American. I don't know the rules of this place. I don't know the signs.

Instead of sleeping, I lie awake on my hard bed, tumbling slowly through the blank silence of a dark city. I could be anywhere. I could be nowhere. If I keep falling, I'll forget my name.

In the morning, we're joined by the two remaining members of our team. The doctor, Kathye, is a lean, glamorous redhead who works rotations in a clinic on the Alaskan slope. Her friend, Jill, from California, is softer, gentler, with long, brown hair and high cheekbones. Both have volunteered in challenging environments before now: Jill in Central America, and Kathye in Vietnam and other parts of Southeast Asia.

While Lama and Zangmo run errands, the rest of us set off for the Forbidden City, which is in the older section of Beijing, a half hour ride from our hotel. I tell the cab driver in Mandarin that we want to go to the *gu gong*—the Palace Museum, as the Forbidden City has been known since the last emperor was ejected in 1924. I smile encouragingly at my companions, a show of confidence that I don't really feel. We could end up anywhere.

Beijing is an appalling, mesmerizing, complex city, its nearly unmanageable contradictions exacerbated by the humidity of mid-July. Though I'm used to Manhattan summers, I'm shocked by the intensity of Beijing's sweltering pollution. It's as if whole lumps of coal or muddy toxins cling to each air molecule and simply to step outside is to invite some sort of fierce contagion.

Taxis here are distinguished by price range. A ride that costs five yuan per kilometer is only moderately cramped, though the cab feels light enough to roll over in a strong wind. Ten-yuan cabs are more solid and familiar, like riding in an old Ford. The three-yuan cabs have rusty bottoms that you can sometimes see through in patches; on the positive side, the drivers tend to treat these fragile vehicles with more concern and are less likely to charge full tilt into traffic, one hand on the steering wheel and the other fixed firmly and continuously on the horn.

We tense as our driver plunges into the ten-lane feud among buses, cars, trucks, taxis, motorcycles, bicycles, and farm vehicles. Other drivers press close, swerve, avoid crashing into us at the last possible second, smashing down on their car horns; our own driver reciprocates in kind. Nothing in his behavior suggests that this dance of death is anything but ordinary.

Halfway between our hotel and downtown Beijing, we pass an area lined with gleaming large hotels and other towering structures in various states of completion. Modernization has completely digested this segment of the city. Here there are no peasants hawking fruit; men and women in tight-fitting business suits move urgently down broad, level sidewalks. Traces of old China are now kitsch: pagodalike awnings and snaking balustrades in the shape of dragons.

The dull red walls of the Forbidden City peer disconsolately over scarlet billboards advertising Coca-Cola. I ask our driver to let us out near the moat that surrounds the palace. Though the water is a fetid, oily, lime green color, several men sit on a stone wall above the water dangling fishing lines among floating lumps of garbage and excrement. Nearby, in a trampled park, a group of schoolchildren in daffodil yellow uniforms screech out patriotic songs. Across the boulevard from the Forbidden City sprawls Tiananmen Square, crowded with pedestrians and tourists waiting in long lines to stare at Mao's body in its glass coffin. An enormous portrait of him overlooks the main gate into the Forbidden City, an ironic sign that the old imperium didn't fall so much as simply change hands.

Thousands of tourists crowd the outer courtyard of the palace complex. While we wait in line for entrance tickets, I quietly rehearse a little speech asking the cost of four tickets. The old woman at the ticket window fixes me with a somewhat zany grin, and I wonder if she's laughing at me or simply relieved that the idiot American hasn't merely tried to make himself understood by shouting in English. At any rate, she pronounces the total very slowly and clearly: *Er bai si shi*, 240 yuan.

I love the thick, almost cottony feel of Chinese paper money, the pale pink and green of the emblems and faces. Paying for things in China feels more like barter than commerce, trading objects beautiful in their own right for goods and services.

Spread out under a thick summer sky, the Forbidden City appears both immense and desolate. Clots of yellow weeds struggle through the dirty marble tiles of ramps and walkways. Tourists crowd the open doorways of the main buildings, jostling each other for a clear view and a quick snapshot of ravaged, unlit interiors. As I squint through the shadows at the emperor's golden throne, I succumb briefly to the same queasy sense of impropriety I'd feel when passing a car accident. The simple fact of picture-snapping tourists gawking at an empty throne guts all sense of gravity and importance.

Above the din, I hear Jill's voice, bewildered, a tone between grief and pleasure. She's telling Martha how hard it is to grasp the change that has taken place in China, and I wonder if she stayed here as a child before the revolution. But no, she's saying she was here in the sixties when everyone was compelled to wear the same type of featureless blue peasant uniforms favored by the chairman: blousy shirts buttoned at the neck and loose trousers. What she can't believe now is the diversity.

"There's so much color," she says, "so many different shapes and styles. That woman over there"—she indicates with her chin—"wearing a pink skirt. Pink! A skirt!"

According to the English-language brochure we received with our tickets, the formal name for the palace is Purple Forbidden City, a name that seems to have nothing to do with the actual muddy red color of the buildings. A paragraph or two later it's explained that the word *purple* is purely symbolic, an imaginative link between the Forbidden City and the palace of the Emperor of Heaven, which was located in the region of the North Star, itself represented by the color purple.

It's an unusual abstraction—color not as color but as idea. As I wander through the immense, symmetrical arrangement of buildings and courtyards, I feel myself becoming sensitized to the symbolism woven into structure of the Forbidden City. Walls are red, representing fire, the emperor's power. Roofs are yellow, representing earth, the basis of form—and by extension, the emperor, the basis of the empire. Hence, when the Empress Dowager Cixi ruled China as regent during a forty-year period that saw the mysterious deaths of several male heirs to the throne, she whispered her commands from behind a yellow screen.

The names of the buildings indicate attitudes rather

than functions. There's the Hall of Supreme Harmony, the Palace of Tranquil Old Age, the Pavilion of Cheerful Melodies. My favorite is the Hill of Accumulated Elegance, a rugged slab of rock artfully carved to symbolize—of all things—a rugged slab of rock. On top stands a small pavilion where the emperor and empress were required to stand once a year on the ninth day of the ninth month to present themselves to a city over which they ruled absolutely but had never entered. For just as the sun's descent from the sky would herald the end of world, so the departure of the Son of Heaven from his earthly court would precipitate disaster. The emperor's palace was also his prison.

After a while, the accretion of signs, the unbending allegory, becomes hallucinogenic. I can almost see through things, catch the form of objects slipping away like veils. The slab of rock is both itself and a symbol of itself; the water in a nearby pond is water and also the idea of water.

The moment passes quickly enough; and as I return to the world of screeching children, camera flashes, and empty Coke cans rolling on cracked stone, I wonder if a phantasmagoric effect has been deliberately triggered. If, far from trapping abstract ideas in concrete forms, the signs and symbols deployed throughout the Forbidden City are meant to turn the mind away from the brute appearance of the common world and toward a luminous swirl of celestial intent.

Which suggests a meticulous brand of irony in the design. I'd always assumed that the name Forbidden City meant simply that commoners were excluded from the palace grounds. But perhaps, like the epithetical *purple*, the term *forbidden* was meant to point beyond the visible. Those who knew the signs would see the Forbidden City, not merely as a series of sacred symbols, but as sacredness itself. The unskilled would know the icon only, living out their lives in the midst of heaven without ever knowing where they were.

Later we walk though the stalls selling trinkets and postcards and sunglasses just outside the Forbidden City, and Kathye buys an umbrella designed like a cat's face. It's bright red with painted eyes and pointed ears poking out of the top. She unfurls her purchase against the Beijing sun, a gesture quaint and at the same time peremptory, Edwardian almost, an echo of corseted ambassadors' wives, the wives of opium importers masquerading as employees of tea companies. A warding gesture, not necessarily uncalled for. We're outnumbered by the surging thousands of Asian tourists fingering cheap scarves, cigarette lighters blazoned with the face of Chairman Mao. Kathye's red umbrella fabric gathers light; the painted eyes stare ahead. Self-mockery can be, at times, a powerful defense.

We cross the boulevard to Tiananmen Square, where

sunlight shoots straight up and merciless from pale concrete slabs. I had been cleaning apartments for a living at the time the massacre occurred; when the news came through, I was dusting knicknacks in a loft in Soho. Now that I'm here, I study the ground for signs, traces of blood, tank tracks, chipped bone. Of course there's nothing.

Jill and Martha stand twenty yards ahead waiting for us. "Mao's tomb is closed for the day," Martha announces.

"But we think he'll still be there tomorrow." This is Jill, brightly enough. She's wilting a little, pressing a can of Coca-Cola to her forehead, the back of her neck. It's ten degrees hotter here out in the open.

At the edge of the square, we climb down to an underpass that runs below the highway. Chinese of all ages line the tiled walls of the cavern, some merely resting, others selling goods of questionable origin and value: cameras, T-shirts, shoes, watches. New lamps for old. When we climb back up to street level, we're in a more decrepit section of the city than we've seen so far, where broken streets creep toward blind alleys and old men stare blankly from the crooked doors of squat, stucco houses.

It's cooler here than in Tiananmen Square and the Forbidden City. The smell of medicinal herbs mingles freely with the thick odors of fried food and fish rotting in the midday heat. At the end of a cul-de-sac, a man sits with his back against a wrought-iron gate of surprisingly delicate design, plunking out an unrecognizable tune on a portable organ. He doesn't have a nose, and he's missing three of the fingers from his left hand: the first leper I've ever seen. As I stoop to drop a few yuan into the cracked bowl in front of the organ, I can't tell if he's grinning a little crazily at us or if his mouth has simply rotted into an open leer.

Artists squat in the street, their work displayed against the seamed walls of old houses. At the entrance to an alley, two boys compete to see who can piss the farthest, while across the way a pair of toothless women in dark blue dresses sit in the shade skinning rabbits. Beside them an old man holds a knife in one hand and the head of a chicken in the other. The headless body, jetting blood, takes a few tentative steps before flopping over, provoking hoarse giggles from the old ladies.

When we get back to the hotel, there's a message from the airport claims office. The man I speak to is very happy to inform me that our luggage has arrived. Unfortunately, he does not have the authority to arrange to have our bags delivered to the hotel, and the person who does have the authority has left for the day. However, he continues, our bags have been piled very neatly in front of the Northwest Airlines luggage carousel, and he's sure that no one will steal anything from such an extremely neat pile.

FOUR

I don't remember who first told me, or why, or under what circumstances. It would have been a fellow student, someone I'd met at a meditation seminar or Tibetan language class, someone riding the train with me between the city and Lama's monastery upstate. I filed the salient facts in memory though. That Padmasambhava, the Lotus-Born himself, had stayed in a cave in the mountains of Nangchen, a region in Kham. A blessed place.

I'd been studying with Lama for almost three years when he invited me to accompany him to Tibet. I'd suffered a couple of setbacks. My relationship of six years had ended; one of my closest friends had died of cancer. I thought I might as well go. Then I remembered the cave.

I thought of the holy man who'd sat there, his journey from a land of sorcerers, shapers of incantations, benders of wind, summoners of rain. After what he'd learned in India, it's likely he no longer believed in their powers as such; even before he left Afghanistan, he'd probably suspected something of the crapshoot nature of priestly sorcerer's tricks, calling down rain for crops, cursing enemies, binding demons. Treating the symptoms of their country's ills, but not the underlying cause.

So he left Afghanistan (or Pakistan, depending on who you read)—part of a caravan probably—trading his magical skills for food, conveyance, the protection of the group. There were horses, carts, elephants maybe; woven materials, spices, metals. Gems possibly. Cautionary tales at night; flickering fires; skins filled with some mulled, intoxicating beverage. Bright implacable stars piercing the unfathomable night.

Then India: hot, lush, and treacherous; streets crammed even then with the sick and the dying; children missing an arm, a leg, abducted into a life of begging, passing their pitiful day's earnings on to one-eyed men unchecked by fear of karmic retribution. Extravagant sights and smells, ululations of grief, hypnotic chanting of Vedic rituals. And beyond the noise a stillness absolute, a sunlit park where the Buddha once sat in rags and held up a flower: his solitary lesson for the day, perhaps the entire year, murmuring, as he caught the recognition in one student's eyes, "This one knows."

In time, the sorcerer from Afghanistan or Pakistan will know, too. The meaning of the flower, the juncture of now and never, this and that, truth and appearance.

Then he will make another journey, far more perilous, over mountains. A journey of some years. Not a quest this time but an answer to the invitation of a king.

For the first time since he left Afghanistan, he'll see snow.

FIVE

You don't look *at* a map of Tibet but *through* it, like studying a layered pattern of stained glass. Each layer has a different shape and color than the rest. A slight difference in some cases, more dramatic in others. The patterns you find will vary according to your mood and what you're looking for.

For example, the country we refer to nowadays as Tibet was, for many centuries, a loose federation of three distinct kingdoms: Tibet, in the west; Amdo in the northeast; and Kham in the southeast. The borders would shift back and forth among the three kingdoms over the years, depending on who had the stronger army, the more ambitious ruler. Twice, all three were swallowed by the Mongol Empire; twice, they formed a vassal state of China.

Before China, before the Mongols, Tibet was an empire in its own right, from the seventh through the ninth centuries, a power to be reckoned with, stretching south into Nepal and west into Turkey, and north along the ancient Silk Road between eastern Asia and the muddy courts of Europe. Before the empire, there were twelve small kingdoms, then twenty-five, then forty. Before the kingdoms there were twelve nomadic tribes. Before the tribes, there were four great clans—or six, depending on which story you're following—ages of legend and heroes riding to war on the backs of pregnant tigresses.

In 1959, the long, complicated argument abruptly ceased. The People's Army completed their occupation, the government fled to India, and Tibet, as a nation, ceased to exist. What remains is a bulge, a growth attached to the western border of Szechuan and split into two unequal portions. The larger has been rolled into the western Chinese province of Qinghai; the smaller is a province called Xizang.

The area we're heading for is called Nangchen, in the southern part of Kham, about three hundred miles from the northern border of Myanmar, which used to be Burma. That's one way to look at it. It's also correct to see Nangchen as a county in the southwestern part of Qinghai, one of the twenty-two provinces that make up China. Qinghai Province is about three thousand miles west of Beijing.

Also: Nangchen is a petty kingdom. There's still a king of Nangchen. I'm told he works in a grocery store. Really he's the nephew of the former king, who died, though no one is sure when. Maybe a few years ago, maybe more; it all depends on who you ask. Memory being another kind of border.

A day and a half after our arrival in Beijing, we're back at the airport, en route to Xining, capital of Qinghai Province. The terminal building is as clogged and noisy as ever, but familiarity makes it easier to preserve a modicum of detachment, through which it's possible to register, consciously, the lack of shops, cafés, newsstands, spaces designed for lingering. Also missing are neon lights, telephone booths, automatic teller machines, shoe-shine stands, the racks of trinkets, the coffee mugs and ashtrays stamped with I LOVE BEIJING. Absence of distraction is a kind of vacuum that would seem to magnify the paroxysmal hysteria.

At the China Air domestic ticket counter, a crisply polite woman in a blue-gray uniform tells us that passengers are allowed only two checked bags apiece at a combined weight not exceeding seventy kilograms. There's a fine for checking more bags, she informs us, and another for exceeding the weight limit. The amounts she quotes are in the hundreds, dollars not yuan.

Apparently, though, no limit applies to the number of

carry-on items we may take on board the plane. A paradox suggesting some dense, unfathomable mystery.

We retreat from the counter to reshuffle the contents of our suitcases, trading sleeping bags and heavy coats for wool socks, boots, and sacks of protein bars. Two gallons of gold paint, gifts for monasteries we will pass on our way through Nangchen, are heaved back and forth before eventually ending up in someone's backpack. We make an odd enough scene—four Americans and two red-robed Buddhists whispering and giggling over a tangle of gutted suitcases—to cause passersby to stop and gape. It takes about half an hour to arrange our belongings so that each person can check two moderately light bags. Even so, we end up having to pay a small fine.

We're the last ones to board the plane, hauling eighteen carry-on bags toward the last row. Only the smallest ones fit into the slotlike bins overhead. The bulging suitcases have to be stacked in the galley, and it's only sheer good luck that the flight attendants find our efforts funny, grinning in their pressed blue suits and white nylons; thick hair pulled back, proper but not too severe. We wrench canvas duffle bags into spaces where our feet should go, our knees propped against our chests when we finally sit, backs flush against the wall because the seats don't recline. Instead, they flop forward. There's no air-conditioning, and it's July, and we don't move from the gate.

Fifteen minutes pass, then twenty, before the flight attendants squeeze down the narrow aisle passing out paper fans. The interior of the plane becomes a field of outsized butterfly wings: green, yellow, ivory, marble-veined, fluttering. Ahead someone laughs, then someone else, a third, then everyone. It's the dawn of religion, spontaneous ecstasy, a stern collective beauty erupting with single force from myriad points of private grief. Then we're moving across the tarmac, down the runway, taking flight.

The city of Beijing folds in on itself and disappears. We pass out of time, suspended in midair as terraced fields beaten yellow by a scalding sun slide eastward down below. The occasional cloud approaches and scuttles away while we remain cocooned inside the white noise of engines, inert, dreaming with our eyes open, digesting nothing.

Immense ridged sheets of pinkish sand unwind outside our windows, crumbling mountains of dry clay, dunes like stunted waves, the frozen cries of ancient mourners. Impossible to say how long it goes on, the Chinese desert.

"How did you get hooked up with them?" This is what Jill asks, sitting next to me, after we take off.

"Them?"

"This particular Buddhist group," she clarifies. "Or is it a sect? The Kagee? The Kaga?"

The actual name is Kagyu, which means "lineage of

the word," specifically, the spoken word, or *ka*—secret instructions whispered by a master in the ear of the disciple, who in turn whispers them to his own disciples, who will whisper them to theirs, and so on over the centuries. *Gyu* means "thread," from which the secondary meaning, "lineage," derives—a word usually preferred by the lamas and their translators over "sect," which suggests a type of conformism incompatible with the spirit of Tibetan Buddhism.

Still, it would be wrong to say there were no differences between the Kagyu and the other three major Tibetan Buddhist lineages: the Nyingma, the Sakya, and the Gelug. On the main point—the Mahayana commitment to liberate all sentient beings from the cycle of suffering—all four schools agree. But the Dharma, the teachings of the Buddha, came slowly to Tibet, an adagio progression lasting more than six hundred years and isolated by time and topography; the early communities of saints each developed specialized interpretations and unique implementations of the basic teachings.

Lost to history are the first contacts between Indian missionaries and Tibetans of the early empire: rumblings and whispers that built to a crescendo in the reign of Songstengampo, a seventh-century king who, perhaps expediently, gave Buddhism a place at court through marriage with the royal houses of Nepal and China. An introduction hardly welcomed by the native priests, an ancient assembly of animists and exorcists, bound in blood to the indigenous gods. Four generations later the royal line produced a true believer, Trisongdetsen, who brought Padmasambhava and the abbot Shantarakshita from India and raised the first of Tibet's great monasteries. Religious fervor receded with his sons though: Ralpachen, assassinated by his brother Langdarma, an apostate murdered by a monk a few years after seizing the throne. A colorful family.

Langdarma's death brought the thousand-year-old dynasty of Tibetan kings to an end. A century and a half of civil wars split the country into a patchwork of petty kingdoms and rival clans. Maybe exhaustion helped foster a return to the Dharma, the emphasis on kindness and eschewing harm. Maybe nostalgia, the cherished flame of lost empire. Maybe despair, the sheer quantity of blood on people's hands.

As the first millennium came to a close, a second dialogue opened up between India and Tibet. Indian masters crossed the mountains to teach in Tibetan monasteries; Tibetan scholars braved the Himalayas and the Karakoram in search of texts, relics, and oral teachings. Forty-five million years earlier, the collision of ancient India and the great northern landmass of Gondwanaland had raised the Himalayas and vaulted the Tibetan plateau three miles into the sky. Now the second wave of Buddhist teaching transformed Tibet's cultural landscape. Monasteries became centers of political power and philosophical training. Buddhist themes rejuvenated

Tibetan art, poetry, and music. Literacy flourished as an entire generation of scholars worked at translating, organizing, and interpreting the massive accumulation of sacred texts carried thousands of miles across perilous mountains and muddy gorges. This second transmission proceeded more or less continuously for more than two hundred years until India fell to Muslim invaders, who burned the libraries, tore down the monasteries and universities, and condemned thousands of monks and nuns to death. By the close of the thirteen century, the Buddha's name had been expunged from the land of his birth, and Tibet had become the guardian of his teaching, the immense, ingenious flowering of medieval India.

At Xining airport, we're the last to deplane, passing our suitcases to the front in bucket-brigade fashion, then climbing down the wobbly stairs to the tarmac. Six or seven young men are loading our things onto dollies, introductions are no doubt made, a mix of Tibetan, Chinese maybe, English possibly; but after the roiling density of Beijing and the uterine compression of the plane trip, the sudden space of Xining compels focus: the clarity of desert sunlight, the broad silence, red mountain shapes against a mirrored sky. Only gradually does human activity reassert its familiar priority, in the center of which two men in particular exert a more specific gravity. One of them is Lama's cousin, Y., a man at the end of the middle age who, though Tibetan by birth, had risen to a position of authority in the government security forces. He looks uncannily like Mao Tse-tung.

The other man is introduced as Bei. At least he keeps pointing to his shirt, which is black, and repeating his name; and then I remember that the Chinese word for "black" is *bei*. So it's unclear if Bei is his real name, his nickname, or simply a convenient alias by which to remember him. He is tall and heavy, nearly twice the size of the chattery young men wheeling our luggage into the terminal building. His presence is immediately comforting, the visibly invisible force of a bodyguard, which is what I assume he is, permanently assigned to Y. the way Secret Service agents are routinely assigned to protect former government leaders in the United States. In any case, his attempt at direct rapport is gratifying, and I reply in halting Mandarin that I'm very happy to meet Bei Xiansheng—Mr. Black—and also (a sentence graven into consciousness by virtue of being in the first lesson of my Chinese language tape) that the plane trip was very smooth.

We follow the younger men through the small terminal and out to the parking lot, where two minivans stand waiting. Most of the luggage, as well as the six or seven young men transporting it, go in one van; we clamber into the other, along with Bei and Y. Past the airport the landscape looks like Tuscany, lithe trees framing undulating fields of flowers and yellow grasses. Buildings along the way are squat and sand-colored, built of stone. Kathye calls out the names of flowers she recognizes, which mean nothing to me.

Our hotel, on the main street of Xining, makes no claims to barring drostitutes from its premises. It becomes the Drostitute Hotel, a name that completely obliterates whatever it's really called. Our rooms are smaller than in Beijing and oddly laid out, with the bathrooms taking up more than half the space. The ceilings are floridly carved, their patterns abruptly bisected by hastily erected separating walls. A tatty brass chandelier over our beds doesn't light; the switch controls a pair of grimy wall sconces. The furnishings are utilitarian: nicked veneer over particle board, hard, narrow mattresses, scratchy blankets. Fleas are likely.

Once our luggage is sorted and distributed, we climb back into the vans and drive down the main street to a complex of government residences about fifteen minutes from our hotel. A uniformed security guard stationed in a cement kiosk at the entrance salutes as we pass into the main courtyard. Children playing in the dusty open area between buildings suddenly stop to gawk at the straggly collection of strangers climbing out of the small vans.

The complex is a warren of concrete walls and harshly lit stairwells, dismal, utilitarian, like government housing anywhere. So the sense of familiarity and comfort inside Y.'s apartment is a surprise: the overstuffed couches around an aging Oriental carpet, the glassed-in porch lined with moribund philodendrons, the smell of frying onions from the kitchen, the murmur of female voices. It's the Bronx, momentarily, it's Queens, except for the half-dozen ebullient conversations in a foreign language swarming around us as we settle in. I long for subtitles to appear on the wall or along the floor molding.

And there are unfamiliar touches, like the ritual of replacing outdoor shoes with indoor sandals. A special pair has been reserved for Lama, of course; the women in our group can slip fairly easily into some of the extra pairs on the porch. Since nothing large enough can be found to fit me, I make do by squeezing into a pair of plastic beach sandals, my toes hanging over one end and my heels over the other, the subject of some mirth among the younger members of the household.

Still, I say *kadrinche*, one of the few colloquialisms I've mastered, meaning not quite thank you, more like "great precious kindness." Y.'s wife shows her teeth and repeats what I said several times over for the benefit the rest of her family, who nod appreciatively, repeating the phrase themselves, a wave of echoes.

While dinner is being prepared, we're served tea—a nearly edible concoction of black twigs, lumps of rock sugar, dried leechees, herbs, and flowers. The cups are small ceramic bowls with lids. Boiling water is poured over the mixture, which has to steep for a few minutes; then you lift the bowl to your lips, using the lid as a sort of filter to keep the larger chunks from escaping. Drinking it produces a glow, a warmth, perhaps caused by the sugar.

Talk swirls around us. A conversation Lama and Y. started on the tarmac shows no sign of flagging. Others join in, leave, form smaller side discussions of their own, arguments, funny stories, eddies of sound, soft teasing accompanied by mock threatening gestures, voices from the kitchen punctuated by clanging pots, voices in the concrete stairwell, children's voices in the dusty courtyard wheedling and chanting. A kind of pulse, a communal history made up in the moment, or of it, life as talk, talk as life, a pattern branching outward from a past beyond reckoning blooming forward to a future unimaginable. In the hushed palatals, the broad fermata of an extended vowel, beats the blood of kings, the march of ancient tribes, holy war, tales to frighten children, remembered noises of a stream at night, a man or woman moaning, wind buckling the side of a tent, the fall of snow.

I'm drinking tea among nomads. Their conversation is their resting place. Tomorrow they'll tear down what they've built today and start all over, fresh.

After that, they'll start again.

SIX

They would have been green, his eyes: pale but luminous, each iris ringed with black. In the pictures painted after his death, he has a thin moustache and wears loose robes of scarlet and gold and a red hat, which is sometimes pointed, sometimes flat, sometimes cone-shaped, like a shell. He's seated, usually, on a throne consisting of a flat moon on a top of a flat sun on top of a broad, flat lotus flower. Each of these things is itself and something else. For that matter, so is he.

There would have been companions, undoubtedly, servants, followers, other missionaries. Also women, though the preferred term is "consorts." They're usually understood to represent something more and less than actual women. One of these will become, as the legend is elaborated, a princess. She'll have a cult of her own, a set of rituals, special songs of incantation. True believers will count her miracles. Does she know this already, squinting at the distant mountaintops like sharks' teeth, infinitely replicating? How much does she suspect?

There would have to have been pack animals of some sort, donkeys, maybe even horses. A three-year trip across the Himalayas would require supplies. Some of the beasts will have died on the way, lost their footing along a ledge, frozen in the night. Some of the companions, too. They would be mourned, naturally, but their deaths would enrich the larger story, the threads of which are held by the man with the green eyes, who will be called Lion someday, the Precious Teacher. Death in his service is more than grace.

Already the legends have begun to collect around him, a dense and luminous coating, a formation of pearl. He was born spontaneously from a lotus. He was raised by a king. He is a form of the Awakened One himself. For eight years he lived in graveyards, taught by angels, fed by gods. He binds and loosens, heals the sick, commands demons. None of it and all of it is true.

Which is why he has been exiled—or invited—to a country of barbarians who paint their faces red when they go to war. Who fear magicians and sacrifice to mountains. A people who think they're descended from a union of god and monkey, who call their country, simply, Home.

Not a pleasant place, but it's where his destiny lies.

His fulfilment. This is one of the things he knows, a measure of the unshakeable certainty that some have read as arrogance. Parties who have had a hand in arranging this invitation from a barbarian king, who are now only beginning to suspect they may have been encouraged in their plans by the man they were trying to defeat. They don't miss him, but they miss the reflected glory of the Lotus-Born.

He stops, and the woman who will become an Indian princess after her death holds up her hand to stop the rest of the party trudging along behind her. She has this power.

Ahead, the Lion considers the nearest peak for a safe pass, reaching out with senses most people have forgotten how to use. Regarding, not space, but time. Currents of possibility, probable outcomes. The fact that even the people closest to him consider this a difficult feat is one of the few things that can still cause him regret. That even those closest to him regard him as a saint.

He starts walking toward the pass he's seen, moving surely, frozen tundra crunching beneath his feet. There are those among the group who will try to step precisely inside his footprints. Empty spaces he leaves behind become relics. The effect he has on people. Men, women, children. Even dogs. His beauty a kind of stillness.

One of them will die tonight on the pass.

SEVEN

Xining is bright, populous, edgy. The light is white and slanted; tawny-colored mountains ring the horizon. Our first morning in the city, Kathye, Martha, and I set out for the department stores we'd passed the night before on our way to Y.'s apartment. We climb on board a wheezing blue bus, dropping change in the coin box. There are supplies to be purchased—batteries, candles, and toothpaste—things we'd forgotten to pack or left inadvertently behind in Beijing. I need to remember shaving cream.

Development in the commercial area seems to have trailed off sometime in the 1940s. Store mannequins imported before the Second World War all have Caucasian features; they have auburn permanent waves, regulation butch-wax haircuts. Their features are blandly generic, like the angels on Christmas cards.

The stores themselves are lit by banks of naked fluorescent lights, which become more glaring the higher you go in the store, where any pretense of seduction is undercut by unpainted cinder-block walls and worn, gouged plank floors. Even so, these stores delight me. The fusty, slightly mildewy odor that permeates the giant disorganized floors invoke memories of the downtown five-and-tens my grandmother used to take me to, magical afternoons marked by such exotic purchases as hairnets and thick corsets.

I buy shaving cream and a map. The map is in Chinese; I only realize when I open it. The place names are indecipherable, but the topography is clear.

In the afternoon we're invited to a banquet with the head of the provincial government. This is not so much an honor as a requirement. In China, as in most places, negotiation demands food, the number of courses served being roughly proportionate to the complexity of the deal to be arranged. Success depends on how well you've eaten and how much you've drunk. A ritual sharing. If the meat is seasoned properly, your request for medical supplies is granted. Each new bottle of brandy means another new school. It's important to linger, to compliment the variety and subtlety of flavors, to make your toasts in the proper turn, to sing uplifting anthems as the meal wears on. A rubbery shrimp, a case of indigestion, can ruin everything. Monumental decisions turn on the texture of fried onions.

We're taken to a pink-walled private room on the top floor of a restaurant, past the goggle-eyed stares of patrons in the main dining area. The room is dominated by a round table crammed with bowls and plates of various sizes. Packs of cigarettes and disposable lighters have been arranged at each place setting. A black-lacquered side table holds at least a dozen decanters of some type of potent and sweet-smelling liqueur. As we settle into our seats, a waitress fiddles with the VCR and television arrangement in the far corner, and suddenly the room fills with a female voice singing Chinese folk songs played out against scenes of happy peasant life. The lyrics roll line by line across the bottom of the screen: Chinese karaoke.

The provincial minister is tall, with an incipient stoop that will probably worsen with age but which now lends him a resigned and almost avuncular aspect. A gravitas. His black bangs hang down over his forehead; the outer corners of his eyes sag. He chain smokes haphazardly, holding his cigarette so that the butt end seems perpetually on the verge of slipping through his fingers while the lit end points precipitously groundward. Three other men accompany him, lesser officials, wan-looking and slightly intimidated. They wear white shirts and neckties; one of them has on thick glasses that don't fit his face.

Conversation proceeds by fits: Chinese to Tibetan, Tibetan to English, and back again. Small talk mostly, barked out with all the desperate cheer of doomed seafarers. We punctuate our remarks with noises associated with demonstrable enjoyment of food. None of our party smokes or drinks alcohol, but we've been joined by a stocky, bearded Australian businessman named Gil. Gil has been in Xining for about ten years, far longer than most Westerners are usually allowed to stay. He wears round, wire-rimmed glasses, a loose Mao shirt, and drawstring trousers. He's been a contact for other Tibetan aid organizations, and has graciously volunteered to serve on this occasion both as translator and as our designated smoker and drinker. His effectiveness in both functions remains unimpaired throughout the meal, a biological miracle given the prodigious amount of food, cigarettes, and alcohol he's required to consume.

Dinner lasts nearly three hours. The food keeps coming: beef tips, pork shreds, chicken, lobster, octopus, shrimp, crab. Curdled in brown sauce, white sauce, sauteed in garlic, oyster sauce. Sides of plum. Broccoli, tomatoes, cucumbers. These are the recognizable items: The more exotic offerings are harder to identify. Tiny eggs that might be quail or pigeon, glistening entrails, eye of newt, skin of toad. Ibex. Civet. The relentless variety of Eastern hospitality.

Our Chinese hosts loosen their ties; they eat and smoke at the same time. At intervals each one must propose a toast. The obligation is passed along the table, only among the men; Lama, as a monk, is exempted. Each time, a small glass of brandy must be downed whole. Gil shows me how to hold the glass so it looks like I'm drinking, then spill the liquor in my napkin. At the end of the first hour my lap is soaking. Then the game changes and instead of toasts there are songs, the singer going from chair to chair handing out full glasses from a tray. The Chinese all sing together, rousing paeans that make them beam and laugh. We sing: "She'll Be Coming Round the Mountain," "Old MacDonald." By the third hour we've run out of songs we know in common; we're onto Christmas carols, which our hosts don't like so much; "Silent Night" is too lugubrious, "Oh, Come All Ye Faithful" too labored. Against our noise, the shrill voice of the taped singing makes an aggressive counterpoint. Lush fields and glowing mountains roll across the TV screen, parks full of happy schoolchildren in yellow uniforms standing at attention, celebrating some manufactured holiday. In the future, their shining faces seem to suggest, all history will be explained in the form of karaoke.

Lama sits calmly throughout, sampling a fried bit of this, a spoonful of that, talking and listening to the provincial minister. Once, in response to some remark, he laughs, a loose rain of random, high-pitched notes, eyes compressed into slits, mouth split in a wide grin.

His laughter, its looseness and delight, is an excruciating lesson. Our hosts may have been the same men who drove tanks into his country, shot people he knew, hung them, burned them alive. I don't know whether to be moved or frightened by his ability to forgive.

The next morning we're up earlier than usual. Lama would routinely wake at dawn to start his morning chanting and meditation practice. About half an hour later, I'd drift toward consciousness on the waves of his soft bass, a rhythmic atonal melody shaped and contained by syllables chanted precisely the same way for a thousand years. Lama would be sitting cross-legged on the bed, his *pechas,* oblong pages of sacred writing, instructions, mantric invocations balanced precisely on his pillow.

He'd smile and nod without breaking rhythm as I blundered in and out of the bathroom and struggled with the hot water thermoses to make tea for both of us. Then I'd sit on my bed trying to emulate his setup as I went about my own morning practice. I find it much more difficult to get my *pechas* to rest quite as easily on my pillow and spend most of the morning hour negotiating between launching a complex visualization of palaces, deific figures, and light rays, and keeping my texts from sliding to the floor.

Now, as we completed our morning practice, Y. and Bei arrive at our door and lead us downstairs; not to the hotel dining room, which hasn't opened yet, but out to the street where the local Chinese Muslims set up cheap, temporary kitchens every morning and afternoon. Kathye, Jill, and Martha meet us outside, bleary but grimly cheerful. Zangmo is sick from the rich food of the night before and won't be joining us.

We sit down to bowls of warm, milky soup and noodles served by round-faced women in white coats and hats that look like surgical caps. In addition to the soup, they load our table with plates overflowing with slightly sodden strips of fried bread and bowls of hot pepper. Most of the other patrons are laborers, thin, heavily tanned men dressed in blue cotton shirts and trousers and blue newsboy caps. They glance surreptitiously in our direction and whisper among themselves smiling if they catch someone's eye.

We eat quickly, following Lama's lead, because we have a long drive ahead, venturing into Tibet, the northernmost tip of Amdo, to visit the village where Y. was born. A new system of water pipes has been installed there, and a new school is being built. We're visiting to observe firsthand the kind of progress that can be made when Western capital, the provincial government, and Tibetan laborers work together for a common goal. The village is an hour's drive away, which actually means it will take about two hours to get there, Tibetan time being more a feeling or agreement than an expression of objective measure.

The dirt road takes us through an undulating succession of terraced farmlands, quilts of bright green-and-yellow squares tossed over a lumpy bed. The road is lined with spindly, white-barked trees and vaguely conical shrubs. Scarves of red dust billow out behind our van as we go higher into the mountains. Occasionally we come up behind a long, three-wheeled, tractorlike vehicle; and Bei, who is driving, duly blasts the car horn until the tractor pulls off to the side of the road and allows us to pass.

Eventually we reach the top of a steep hill, where we pass an odd stone structure with several strings running from the top to the ground, all lined with faded pennants flapping in the breeze. It looks like a collapsed windmill, but in fact it's a shrine to one of the local gods, many of whom were "converted" from unruly demons to protectors of Buddhist teaching the way local gods of Dark Age Europe were recycled into patron saints. The protectors remain a largely unruly lot, requiring regular offerings in order to ensure their allegiance and to inhibit their passion for causing landslides and earthquakes. As we pass the shrine, Martha whispers that we have now officially passed into Tibet.

At the top of the next hill, we stop to look down on the village where Y. was born. As he describes the layout below, Lama translates, telling us how more than ten kilometers of pipes now direct water from the springs in the surrounding foothills into every home in the village. This saves hours of hauling water by hand everyday. At one edge of the village we can see the clearing for the new school and part of its foundations already laid.

We drive to the construction site and getting out of the van I surrender to an unabashedly tourist impulse, hauling out my camera in hopes of preserving for some imagined posterity the wonderful *uniqueness* of native Tibetan life. The *poignance* of the children who swarm around us, staring wonderingly from their dark, planar faces. Their faded, baggy clothes. One boy has on a denim jacket with a patch-sized white bunny below the lapel; another wears a dirty, pale blue sweatshirt depicting a litter of cartoon puppies squirming cutely beneath a logo of Western-style letters that spell no recognizable word. A wall of mud and stone surrounds the site, and two young girls in pink sweaters crawl over a mound of rocks near the perimeter. Beauty of a raw, complex sort. These children don't smile; even the youngest look like anxious adults.

After the school, we move on to Y.'s family home, which is organized in a U-shape around a stone courtyard. Whitewashed walls, bleached by the sun to the color of ancient bones, are relieved here and there by splashes of paint, red around doorways, dark green around windows. Intricately carved and painted beams frame the exterior. Wild flowers in various colors grow directly out of the mud roof. Inside, packed earth floors have been immaculately swept. Before any of the ritual hospitalities begin, we're favored with a demonstration of the recently installed spigot, from which running water miraculously flows. The kitchen is just a partitioned area between a large platform bed and another raised platform for eating. Two women in heavy, dark robes cook lunch over a tile-lined stove very low to the ground; the excess heat flows through a kind of tunnel to warm the platform bed.

The dining area is lit by a large window framed in bright red-and-ochre-painted wood. A low table has been set out. Lama sits at the head, below the window, while the rest of us crowd around on either side. Piles of *balop*, pan-cooked bread, have already been laid out, along with a plate of chunks of bright yellow yak butter, which is fresh and therefore edible, with a rich, cheesy taste.

Tea is poured—not the elegant, sugared drink we had in Xining, but a potent decoction of black twigs. The bitterness is mitigated somewhat by ice-cream-scoop-sized dollops of yak butter. Moments later, two cord-thin men with leathery, dark skin—the village schoolteacher and the village doctor—slide bowls of roasted yak, still on the bone, onto the table. One of the phrases I have practiced is *sha sa migu*, "I don't eat meat." A vital bit of information. I point to Kathye, saying we, *narangtso*, don't eat meat. Accordingly, we're handed triple portions of fresh goat's milk yogurt, topped by lilliputian tubers, which Lama explains are Tibetan potatoes. "Very good for the digestion," he says. Then adds, a whoops, an afterthought, "Don't eat too many."

We're given seconds, thirds, even fourths of every dish, and not understanding the protocol or wishing to offend, we accept as graciously as possible. Afterward it becomes crucial to ask for the bathroom. One of the old men, I'm not sure if he's the doctor or the schoolteacher, leads me outside. At the edge of the courtyard, he points across the road to a mud wall where a burlap curtain hangs in front of a sort of doorway built into the wall. Behind the curtain is a small, squarish room with no roof and a pit in the middle of the dirt floor. It's sheer luck that I'd stuffed a wad of toilet paper in my pocket before leaving Xining. However, I'm not yet adept at squatting, and my insides balk. The two-hour ride back to the city feels like a kind of punishment.

We return in time to brush off the dust and change into our good clothes for a second official banquet with a larger number of local officials and several women, wives or mistresses. Perhaps a couple of drostitutes. The presence of women has a tempering effect on the amount of liquor consumed, as well as the decibel level at which the karaoke videos are played. Still, the hours pass slowly, occupied mainly with finding creative ways of restating that China is very beautiful, Xining is very big, the mountains are very tall. At the end of the dinner, the bureaucrats and their wives appear just as relieved to conclude this awkward effort at detente as we are.

"I think we just came through the *bardo* of overeating," I groan, lying on my back on the floor of Jill and Kathye's room, regarding my abdomen with a feeling between awe and horror.

"What do you mean, *bardo?*" Jill asks.

"It's a kind of state, actually more of an in-between state. The word means 'gap.'"

"Like suspended animation?"

"Sort of."

I feel as if I'm caught in a suspended state right now. I feel like a walrus, blubbery, a beached whale. Not a noodle, not a grain of rice, seems to be digesting. I'm sure I can feel oblong, lumpy snow peas pressing against my skin from the inside.

"The *bardo* is where you go when you die," Martha says. She's one of the lucky ones, able to sit upright against a wall. She looks scrubbed, American in the sense of appearing very open, trusting. Impressions register quickly on her face.

"Oh, good"—Kathye comes out of the bathroom after changing into green scrubs, her sleepwear—"no heaven or hell."

"Not strictly true," I reply. "There are twelve hells. Six hot, six cold. Also some ancillary hells. Side tunnels."

"Eighteen," Martha says.

I manage to turn my head to look at her. "Is it eighteen altogether or eighteen ancillaries?"

"Eighteen altogether."

"They have names, too: the Hell of Molten Lead, the Hell of Sharp Knives, the Cesspool of Rotting Corpses, the Road of Razors."

The diverse elements of Tibetan Buddhist philosophy, epistemology, and practice are organized into a catalog of names and numbers, a portable mnemonic system, useful for nomads, warring clans. Eighteen hells, six kinds of beings, five unpardonable acts. Ten freedoms. Six *bardos.* 84,000 teachings. A system of memorization the Tibetans call "writing on the ribs." You never knew when a band of Mongol warriors or rival monks was going to march up and burn down your monastery. There wasn't always time to pack up your scriptures and get out of Dodge.

Kathye pulls down her blanket and lies gingerly down on her bed. "I love nonviolence," she says.

"How can there be only six *bardos?*" Jill asks, "if there are eighteen hells?"

"Hell isn't a place you go after you die; it's a place you're born."

The *bardos,* on the other hand, are constantly cycling. Or rather, the individual mind is always cycling through the *bardos:* The Bardo Between Birth and Death, the Bardo of Dreams, the Bardo of Dying. The process described in *The Tibetan Book of the Dead,* the *Bardö Tödöl,* more precisely translated as "Liberation Through Hearing in the *Bardo.*" A treasure left behind by Padmasambhava in his travels across Tibet.

After death comes the Bardo of Reality, an experience of light, not cozy but terrifying, like a nuclear blast. This is the Clear Light of Mind, the essence of your being, experienced in its totality without ego, without mitigating filter. A reality glimpsed in deep meditation. But even with practice, most individuals can't take the Bardo of Reality. It's unbearable, the naked mind, a density unimaginable. Better to pass out, to sink into darkness, escape the light before burning up in it.

No one anticipates waking afterward in the Bardo of Becoming: anxiety in its pure state, a kaleidoscopic rotation in which the disembodied ego suffers the effects of freezing winds, tearing rain, the abrupt manifestation of fanged and bloody monsters. If you've meditated deeply in life, you may be able to recognize these experiences as projections of your own mind, reflections of the Clear Light, like the colored rays that appear when light is shined through a crystal. Once recognized, the terrors cease, the mind is freed from the cycle of the *bardos.* The habit of incarnation is hard to resist though, and the disembodied ego, overcome by fear and fatigue, will usually seek shelter, even if it means squeezing inside a crack in a stone, passing through the Bardo of Rebirth back in the Bardo Between Birth and Death, only now as an ant, or a centipede. A maggot.

If you behaved badly in your previous life, the force of habit will drive you toward rebirth in one of the hell realms. Or maybe one of the other unhappy states: the

animal realm or the realm of hungry ghosts, pitiful creatures with bloated stomachs and pin-sized throats. After
burning through your bad karma, maybe you'd pass
through death, reality, and becoming again to spend the
next Bardo Between Birth and Death in a higher state:
the Realm of Happy Gods or the Realm of Demigods. If
you achieve the right balance of positive and negative
karma, you may end up in the human realm, where the
experience of suffering is matched by the opportunity
and the incitement to study the Dharma and break out
of the cycle altogether.

"First you're born," Martha says. "Then you die. Then
you're born; then you die. Then you're born; then you
die."

Jill replies that it sounds exhausting.

"It is." Martha's face begins to flush "It's the first thing
the Buddha taught: Life is suffering. That's the First No-
ble Truth."

"Oh, God, are there eighteen of those, too?"

"Only four."

Jill groans.

"The first is suffering," Martha says, having apparently
succeeded in writing a few details on her ribs. "Next is
the cause of suffering. Third is the release from suffering,
and fourth is the path of release."

"Which is eight-fold," I add, "just to liven things up."

"Those are the four *bardos?*"

"No, six *bardos,* four truths."

" 'And a partridge in a pear tree,' " Kathye sings. "That's what we should have sung tonight. I don't think we can sing "Old MacDonald" anymore; we always mix up the animals."

Tibetan Buddhism, with its carefully articulated systems, precise categories of experience, is, on a certain level, a language of perception: life as an interval between birth and death; dream as an interval between sleep and waking. It's a language preoccupied with boundaries, which would seem to oppose the Western—or, at least, American—focus on expansion, limitless possibility. We don't like to think about boundaries; we're diminished by endings. So perhaps we'll work on four or five different things at once, staggering deadlines so that we're never left without a project. If we keep busy, we'll never suffer, we'll never die. A moving target is harder to hit than one that is sitting still.

Later that night a woman knocks on the door of the room I share with Lama. I recognize her from the first night at Y.'s apartment, though I'm not sure whether she's a relation or merely a friend. She's stout, wearing a shiny, olive green–colored skirt that covers her knees and a drab blue cardigan over her blouse. She bobs her head in greeting to Lama, who is sitting on the other side of the room deep in conversation with Y. and two other men. Then she hooks me by the arm, babbling. I recognize a few of the words, one of them being *injike*—the Tibetan term for "English"—but I'm hopelessly out of my depth.

Lama translates. "She wants you to go her house," he says. "You hear her daughter speak English."

It's my own fault, the result of my liberal, if mangled, sprinkling of Tibetan and Chinese over dinner our first night at Y.'s apartment. So now I'm a linguist. The men sitting with Lama crane their necks, nodding encouragement. Lama says, "Go."

The woman's home isn't far from the hotel, a ground-floor apartment with furniture vaguely reminiscent of Danish modern. Photographs of snowy mountains and two or three cheap silk paintings of Buddhist figures decorate the walls. Before anything else we have to share several cups of flavored tea. My bladder by now is awash with the stuff, and the first blush of delight has worn off. After five minutes, I've exhausted my repertoire of colloquial Tibetan. All the rest I know is liturgical.

The awful silence ends finally when her daughter, a sweet-faced ten year old in blue nylon pants and a pink blouse, enters the room. At her mother's prompting she sits shyly beside me on the sofa and starts reading aloud from a school textbook, enunciating with the toneless perfection associated with furious concentration on sounding correct. Her proficiency far surpasses my own ability to pronounce Tibetan.

When she's finished, I imitate my Chinese language

teacher back in New York, smiling raptly while brightly shouting, *Due la,* "Very good." Because it's expected, I point to a couple of words on each page and pronounce them more precisely. The girl repeats them back to me, slowly, carefully.

Then something unexpected occurs, an exchange not grounded in the words we're parroting back and forth. A seeing. A speaking to each other *through* words, but not necessarily *in* them. Communication as subject. It's like reaching through a mirror and finding, not the airy nothing of my own reflection, but a form of surprising solidity and warmth, at once familiar and terrifyingly distinct. The effect is profoundly disorienting.

The streets of Xining are dark when I return to the hotel. A few people sit on their front stoops cooling themselves with paper fans. A corner newsstand glows with bluish neon, glass shelves sparsely clustered with pink- and blue-wrapped candy. The hotel is easy enough to find. Even so, I'm lost. Even in the dark, with the scratchy blanket pulled up as far as it can reach, I'm no longer sure where I am.

EIGHT

The next day we leave for Kham, about four hundred miles southwest as the crow flies. We're not traveling by crow, however, but by bus, a longer and more intricate journey.

At the Xining depot, a scrawny man in a drab green uniform runs toward us, waving his hands and screaming. Bei swings from the front seat of the van and strides toward the protesting guard. He stands a good foot and half over the guard and outweighs him by at least fifty pounds. And while the smaller man continues to scream and wave his hands, Bei calmly shuffles through his wallet until he finds the most appropriate card, the one identifying him as an elite member of government security forces. The little officer keeps up the screaming and waving right up until the moment he reads the ID card, at which point he abruptly stops and motions our driver to proceed through the gate.

It's easier to appreciate the guard's stop-and-scare tactics once we're inside the bus depot parking lot, where whatever space hasn't been delegated to waiting buses has been homesteaded by compact masses of prospective travelers. A diverse group, some in business suits and tight dresses, others in worn uniforms, violently colored T-shirts, peach nylon skirts. Huddling protectively around misshapen boxes and ominously fragrant bags of edible things too terrible to contemplate. Children wander unattended from group to group, the more ragged ones begging, their perseverance unchecked by rejection, angry gestures, simple disregard. Vendors circulate, hawking candy, beer, fruit, roasted corn, Coca-Cola, a sugary orange drink called Jian Li Bao. Sidling up to bus windows, they offer riders a last-minute chance to provision themselves against the verge of not quite movement, an air of expectancy and hopelessness, the menace of a too-bright sun.

A bus coughs and lumbers from its berth, dragonlike, a prehistoric grandeur in its ponderous motion, making for the narrow concrete ramp that is both entrance and exit to the station. There's a pause, a collective inbreath; then the waiting groups hoist their bags and boxes and regroup a few feet to the right or left of their original positions. The scrawny children and vendors recommence their efforts to wheedle a few coins where they can.

White sun assaults the battered asphalt, the scene wavers, an image unable to gel.

A second van pulls up behind ours and Y. steps from the passenger seat. The crowd that has gathered to watch the spectacle of a group of nervous Westerners unloading an absurd amount of luggage parts before him. He talks to the bus driver, quietly, earnestly. Bei, meanwhile, directs the same young men who'd met us at the airport to load our things onto the bus. The driver orders passengers who have already settled onboard to get out, a turn of events they accept blandly enough, though some regard us with a cool sort of pity, our concern for priority such evident bad manners. Barbarians, how can we know any better?

It takes a good quarter-hour to pile our luggage in the back of the bus, another fifteen minutes for us to settle into our assigned bunks. Each is about the size of a child's coffin, lined with some sort of pale, dusty green canvas. After rolling up the dingy blanket provided, I squeeze into the window seat; then Martha slides in next to me. Lama hops into the upper bunk directly above, followed by Zangmo, who has assumed the fiercely protective mask reserved for times when strangers get too close to Lama. Kathye and Jill claim a pair of lower bunks directly across the aisle from us.

Boarding occurs in spurts. Lama buys a few ears of roasted corn and a warm bottle of Coca-Cola from one of the strolling vendors. Other passengers buy beer or watermelon or long sticks of frozen, sweetened juice. Despite the large no-smoking symbol prominently displayed at the front of the bus, roughly half of our fellow travelers light up. The bus fills with blue, curling smoke, shifting shapes of dragons, snakes, petals. From time to time enormous heads of dried sunflowers are slid through the open windows. The seeds are a staple of the Tibetan diet, but I've never before seen them plucked directly from the flower. Gradually, the aisle of the bus becomes littered with broken seed pods. When completely stripped, the flower gets flung like an empty plate from the bus window.

Zangmo calls down news, good and bad. The bad is that the trip to Yushu will apparently last twenty-two hours instead of fifteen. The good is that the bus driver is Y.'s nephew, which means we can be relatively certain of stopping if the need becomes critical. Also, he'll keep an eye on the luggage.

The bus rumbles to a start about an hour after we've boarded, backs out of its resting place, squeezes through the narrow exit ramp. Behind us, on either side, the crowd shifts, resettles, huddling protectively over their boxed possessions. The peddlers take up their cries. A child manages to pick a wallet, and another lifts some fruit.

We drive for an hour and a half then pull into a sort of market square, somewhere south. The names have disappeared. We follow Lama into a Muslim restaurant, where he orders for us steaming bowls of noodles swimming in a spiced sauce that manages to taste both hearty and delicate at the same time, our last meal before we get to Yushu. After that we wander through the stalls of cheap goods, brass ritual objects, postcard-size prints of sacred images, T-shirts, prayer flags, plastic sunglasses, thin socks. Rugs.

There's a public bathroom, a long, wooden building; one side for men, the other for women. Even before going in, I know it's a mistake, but the confirmation is somehow necessary. The last public toilet in China. The floor is a series of evenly spaced wooden rungs splattered with shit and slick with urine. Below, a kind of fetid archaeology, wet and rotting, a record of migratory movements. There's no place to step without establishing an intimate rapport with history, with the viscera of strangers. I step back into the open air, unable to rise to the challenge.

Some ten or fifteen new passengers join us as we prepare to leave. Many of them seem to have some military or security connection. They wear uniforms, at least, new ones, clean ones, and commandeer for themselves the first row of bunks in the bus. The people who had been sitting there relocate to the back of the bus and the aisles. The bus makes a wide arc around the square, then pulls through the narrow entrance back out onto the open road.

After dusk, the chattering conversations in various parts of the bus drop to a low murmur, then fade to a thick, grumbling, dormitory silence. The bus rocks rhythmically along the road, chugging higher and higher through the mountains. I don't want to sleep. I don't want to miss any of this. Once in a while the driver stops; we step out into keen air that tastes almost metallic and enjoy the guilty pleasure of peeing openly in the dark. The waves of pale tundra under an ice blue moon define a mythic passage, an underworld, a land of shades, where names and faces are forgotten. A bleakness so severe as to verge on beauty.

At dawn mountains can be seen in the distance, stumpy and crooked like rows of an old man's teeth. We drive straight toward them, hardly noticing the gradual incline until we've reached the top and make a sharper, more obvious descent. In the distance we see another range of mountains, this time purple, with rounded peaks more noticeable against the brightening sky. We slide too quickly down steep valleys of piercing green then head up into the mountains again, hardly noticing the incline until we reach the top and begin yet another sharp descent.

In the distance, another range of mountains.

The pattern repeats itself a fourth time, a fifth, a sixth. Eventually I surrender to a sort of exhausted despondency, eyes burning from lack of sleep and from the unending stream of cigarette smoke sweeping back from the front of the bus where the military officers sit chain-smoking, crushing their butts in the aisle. On and off one of the soldiers stares at me, a man of middle age, seamed face, receding hairline. Chinese, not Tibetan. It's easy to tell because of the narrowness of his features, the bones pronounced, fine, as though they've been pinched and fired. Impossible to read the meaning in his stare. Possibly boredom. The number of times he's taken this ride, from nowhere to nowhere in a country that does not exist. He drops his cigarette in the aisle, uses the toe of his right foot to crush it without looking. This is what cats do, stare at each other until one or the other blinks or turns away. It's a way to establish dominance without drawing blood.

I blink.

I see no reason to upset the order of things.

At full morning an odd speck on the side of the road ahead catches my attention. The shape gradually defines itself as we drive nearer, the oddly crumpled central heap assuming a density, strings of pennants trailing from the top to the ground, flapping in the breeze, a shrine to a local god.

"Is this it? Are we in Kham now?"

From the bunk above me, Lama's voice, weary and amused, "Yes, this is Kham."

We draw close to the shrine, then past it. I prepare for

magic, momentousness, the potency of sacred ground. Instead, our driver inserts a tape into the dashboard cassette player, and cuts the silence with a Carpenters song: "Every Sha Na Na." This is followed by "I Just Called to Say I Love You," the theme from *Love Story*, and "Endless Love."

What an appalling contrast, swooping down from the heights on the wings of cheesy love songs.

In self-defense I fall asleep.

Gondwanaland

NINE

There was a void in the beginning, before trails of vapor from the ten directions streamed together to form a pale blue sphere of solid air called the Cross of Winds. Above the Cross of Winds appeared an ocean, millions of miles wide and millions of miles deep, on which rose the foundation of the universe: a golden expanse, flat as the palm of a hand. In the center of the gold expanse rose Mount Meru, or Mount Sumeru if the text requires a longer line verse: poetry being that much easier to recall than prose and people being creatures not so much of habit but of rhythm, enthralled by drum beats, heart beats, the steady tap of rain.

This primal world divided and grew like a cell. Seven mountains suddenly materialized around Sumeru, and seven oceans roiled out of nowhere to lap around the shores of the seven mountains. Five heavens appeared next, one on top of the other: The Heaven of the Gods of the Thirty-Three Realms, Conflict-Free Heaven, Joyful Heaven, the Heaven of Self-Evident Happiness, the Heaven of Those Who Triumph Over The Manifestations of Others. Above, below, and intersecting these heavenly abodes appeared worlds of desire, worlds of pure form, and dimensions of formlessness, each characterized by a different mode of experience.

The World of Desire, for example, experienced generally as endless oscillation between pleasure and pain, is said to include the six major categories of experience or realms: the Hell Realm, the Hungry Ghost Realm, the Animal Realm, the Human Realm, the Realm of Demigods, and the Realm of Gods.

From which lively process of division and subdivision, the universe emerged, emerges, dissolving continuously in its own inventive play. Four continents, each distinguished by a particular shape and color, encircle the great mountain in the center of the universe. Our earth is part of the southern continent, which is blue, shaped like a pair of wings. Its name is Dzambuling, the southern continent. In its exact center, so the story goes, lies India, referred to by the anonymous authors of Tibet's cosmology—the blind poets, the village chiefs—as a land of treasures, a canopy of purest silk. A detail that suggests that this creation story, which locates paradise, not in some mythic region, but in the country next door, may not be native to Tibet.

Conquering armies deface temples, topple the mon-
uments of defeated kings, ransack the tombs of ancestors. This is to be expected; the local gods must be
humiliated, their potencies dispersed. But native tales of
the beginning, an imaginative link between the local
scene and paradise, tend to keep on living underground,
gathering power in secret among old wives, children, the
dying, and the mad. They become the pungent procre-
ative loam out of which a culture reinvents itself. So how
did India become the Eden of Tibet's creation tale?

A younger son of a younger son, an inconvenient prince
of northern India, marked for poison or a wandering
arrow. Deformed, too, according to one version of the
legend—cast as a bad omen into the Ganges and later
rescued by peasants. A Hindu Moses, fleeing north for
who knows what reason—adventure, territory. His flight
would have occurred in the third or fourth century
B.C.E., a period of some fluctuation among the Indian
ruling class.

Like Moses, this prince or minor functionary descends
from a sacred mountain on the Tibetan side of the Himalayas, which only intensifies the shock of his Aryan oth-
erness: his height, the narrow mold of features, the dusky
skin. The natives he meets are stocky, with broad features, spatular hands. Nomads and occasional farmers.
If they understand his appearance as miraculous, a de-

scent from heaven on a cord of light, why argue? Propaganda is a necessary adjunct of power: a member of the ruling caste, even a deformed one, would know this. Just as he would know enough casual magic to send the local shamans packing and make the local chieftains bow.

The timing is right, too. Twelve petty kingdoms at war with each other are catnip to the more organized powers forming on all sides: Persia, China, India. The Aryan hunchback welds a small but determined empire from the feuding domains, a threat to the Ch'in Dynasty in the east, the Persian Empire in the west, the Nepalese in the south. He becomes a hero, carried on the shoulders of his new subjects, from which derives his new, Tibetan name: Nya-tri, Neck Enthroned.

Though fruit trees, grapes, and figs grow in the southern reaches of the new empire, the bald, airless, northern regions are so dry that snow barely has a chance to form before it evaporates in midair. Mountains sulk along the horizon like fat, murderous children; stars split the sky at night, invading armies from a bulging otherworld. An elemental isolation permeates the empire, a kind of soot that gathers in your pores, your lungs, mingles with your spit, mixes havoc with your seed. Though you've risen higher than you ever could have as the hunchback son of a second son, you still find yourself dreaming of home, of India, a land of treasures, a canopy of purest silk.

The hand of the son who closes your eyes for the last

time will stink of rancid butter; his breath will be heavy with the meat of slaughtered yak. Still, he will rule the empire you created and he will need your gods, your legends, your knowledge of the universal order to steer by. So that someday he, or his son, or his son's son, will complete your journey, arrive back where you started, and call it home.

TEN

At eleven in the morning, our bus pulls to a stop in a public square sparsely occupied by grimy children, old ladies, itinerant monks. Two-story huts, whitewashed at some point in the distant past, line either side of the road: beer halls, shops selling brass trinkets, cheap socks, jars of neon-bright jelly.

Somewhat tentatively, Martha asks why we've stopped.

"Just wait," Zangmo replies. "In a few weeks, you'll think of this as a bustling metropolis."

Yushu City is the capital, not only of Yushu County, but also of a larger area called Yushu Prefecture, one of six administrative districts in Qinghai Province. Theoretically a hotbed of municipal activity.

A tall monk named Kagi and a small, wiry man called Jampay push through the small crowd of children, beggars, and leering teenage boys that has collected around the bus. They have enlisted five or six young men to help with the luggage, the boxes of medical supplies; and by means of gestures and proximal attempts to communicate in Tibetan, we devise a system for passing smaller articles through the back windows of the bus and moving larger items out the front. The luggage is piled into two waiting jeeps, one of which belongs to Jampay. The other belongs to Rigdzin, a man in his late twenties with shoulder-length hair. In addition to a *sham tab,* or monk's skirt, Rigdzin wears a pale yellow button-down shirt, a camel-colored blazer, and wraparound sunglasses. It's unclear whether his wardrobe is a statement or merely a felicitous accident.

Crammed in the jeeps, we wind our way up a steep dirt road, switching back and forth at precipitous angles. After a while it's impossible to maintain a coherent idea of our route. Narrow streets branch off the main road, skittering between khaki-colored walls decorated with small, painted shapes: red squares, blue circles, yellow triangles. Now and then an iron gate or a window breaks the monotony. The sides of the road are littered with soda cans, food wrappers, scraps of metal. Flat roofs peek over the walls, tilting at odd angles.

"There was a crooked man," Jill murmurs next to me, "who had a crooked house."

"On a crooked street."

From around the bend ahead comes a woman draped

in heavy black wool, a face older than the Gutenberg Bible, arm-in-arm with another woman, younger, her daughter or granddaughter, who wears a lump of coral the size of a baby's fist pinned to her hair. We stop to let them pass, and the old woman grips the side of the jeep with surprising force, muttering and bowing her head so Lama can bless her. Her clothes reek of yak butter, an unmistakably animal aroma, pungent, alive.

A few more turns in the road, and we arrive at Jampay's house, a two-story building with painted wood trim along the roof, doors, and window frames. There's a dirt courtyard, a pair of reedy flower beds, a tall, brick wall with an iron gate. A knot of six or seven people stand in front of the house holding white scarves, *katas*, to hang around our necks as tokens of respect.

As guests of honor, we're given bedrooms on the second story, which are not shared with dogs or livestock. They're arranged in a line along a wide concrete balcony, reached by means of a wooden ladder inserted through a hole cut in the balcony floor. Because of the angle at which the ladder is set, you have to pitch abruptly forward on the last few rungs in order to avoid slamming your head against the underside of the balcony. A lesson learned through painful experience.

Martha and Zangmo share one room, Kathye and Jill another. Lama is led to a special chamber that houses an intricate hand-painted shrine and a bed piled with thick, wool rugs. I'm given a kind of living room outside

Lama's bedroom, it being understood that as the male member of the entourage I must serve in some attendant capacity. Like the other rooms, it has whitewashed walls and a floor of tamped earth. The walls are lined with plank benches draped with wool rugs of deep maroon and gold. A window opens onto an edenic view of dark green hills, tier after tier, glazed by the white luster of midday sun.

As soon as I put my bags down, I reach for my camera, compulsively documenting the view as seen through my window, my room as seen from the doorway, the courtyard as seen from the balcony. A bowl of pale yellow butter on the top shelf of a lacquered cabinet. Jampay's sister, as she lays out lunch for us on a plank in my room, becomes a subject. Also the puffed loaves of pan-baked bread, the strips of boiled yak meat with tufts of hair feathering the edges, the kettle of rice big enough to sit in.

After lunch, Jampay's son, Tsewong, a ten year old with a world-class plug of snot in one nostril, decides I need to take a tour of the immediate vicinity. The first point of interest is the sitting room, distinguished from the other rooms in the house by several intriguing features. There is a sofa and an easy chair, for example, both covered in thick, tattery plastic, and a refrigerator in the far left corner of the room. The most distinctive element, though, is the television set, fairly new, perched on the widest shelf of a kind of hand-painted wooden hutch. A dark, saclike object, which on closer inspection turns out to be Jampay's mother, is sitting on the sofa watching a broadcast of the *taqyuk kuchen,* or "horse festival," held for a full week each summer in one of the counties of Yushu Prefecture. There are races and stunt riders, weight-lifting contests, and folk dancing. Tsewong tells me a lot of people drink beer and throw up.

On our way through the courtyard he shows me the outhouse, inconveniently located twenty yards from the main building: mud walls high enough to preserve a reasonable sense of privacy, a door of bound twigs, which closes after a fashion. There's nothing to sit on, naturally, just a hole in the dirt floor. The principal challenge would seem to involve maneuvering past the family dog, tied to a stake several feet from the outhouse. To ensure an optimum degree of ferocity, the animal is kept in an agitated state, frequently pelted with stones, its neck bound uncomfortably tight with rope. The thought of encountering the family Cerberus on a nighttime run to the outhouse doesn't inspire comfortable thoughts.

Out the gate Tsewong and I meander uphill for a while, passing other houses where laundry hangs limp on twisted lines and weeds grow out of dirt roofs. Twelve thousand feet above sea level, it's harder to breathe than I would have imagined, and the lack of oxygen induces a peculiar kind of vertigo. A flattening and crowding of the field of vision, a surgical brightness in which commonplace objects seem to hint at a deeper, more complicated meaning. A battered bicycle leaning against a gate. An abandoned shoe. Tire tracks baked in dried mud. Contradictory signs of fragility and eternity.

When we reach open ground above the houses, Tsewong runs ahead up a hill, picking his way among chunks of dirt and rock. I labor behind, the Little Engine That Just Barely Could, certain that something vital will burst from the exertion of climbing: an artery, a lung.

The view from the top of the hill is Olympian, however, inspiring naked awe. Under a lapis sky, a random geometry of green hills encircled by concentric rings of pale mountains extend gray, blue, purple, one beyond the other like gargantuan ripples of sheer, not quite solid, material; below, a precise diorama of flat-roofed houses, tiny gardens, doll-sized people.

From where we stand, we can see a woman step out of her house with a baby in one arm and a wicker basket in the other. She sets the basket on the ground and with her free hand begins plucking clothes from the line stretched across the yard. The baby never squirms.

We watch a man emerge from a trap door in the top of a roof, then turn and squat to lift a bucket handed up through the trap. He carries the bucket to one end of the roof and starts spilling water back and forth in a rough line, moistening the dirt. When he runs out of water, he returns back across the roof to where another bucket sits waiting at the edge of the trap door. He reaches the empty bucket down through the hole then carries the full one to the edge of the roof and begins pouring water where he'd left off.

I take a photograph of Tsewong standing in front of an enormous boulder carved with mantras. A mani stone it's called, after the mantra written on it: *Om Mani Peme Hung*, sometimes translated as "Jewel in the Lotus" or "Hail to the Lotus-Jewel." Scholars have produced volumes arguing for and against a given version, but the exact meaning has never been pinned down. According to Lama, knowing the literal meaning of a mantra would be a distraction: It's the sound, the activity of repetition that catalyzes experience, deepens meditation, stills the mind.

After I take his picture, Tsewong begs me to let him photograph me. I agree, nervously, not knowing enough Tibetan to explain how to operate the camera. Of course he wants to take a second picture, then just one more. He flashes a wheedling grin—just one more. He concentrates furiously on choosing a subject, focusing, sliding his finger across the top of the camera to find the shutter button.

Months later, when I develop pictures of my Tibet trip, Tsewong's photographs make an interesting series. In most of them, his fingers are spread across the camera lens, while a film of dust or grease on the lens makes it hard to distinguish between foreground and background. As a result, the purple mountains, the mud brick houses perched precariously on craggy hills, are reduced to slivers, shards of a broken landscape cradled in the hands of a ten-year-old boy. In one picture, the shards are arranged in a way that almost resembles the petals of a stylized flower.

Foreigners entering strictly controlled areas of China for the first time are required to visit the local tourist bureau and fill out forms. Accordingly, later in the afternoon, Zangmo, Martha, and I are taken back down the hill to register our group at the Yushu County office. The others don't have to come; we have their passports, from which we can copy the information needed for the government forms.

The regional tourist office in Yushu is tucked away in the back of a concrete building, across a dry bit of lawn, up a flight of dingy, badly lit stairs. The reception room is spare, crammed with scarred wooden desks, wooden file cabinets, slatted benches—a setting that evokes *film noir:* Barbara Stanwyck should be standing in the doorway clutching a small, pearl-handled revolver; Peter Lorre should be lurking in a corner; everything should be black and white.

As a child of the Cold War, I expect the bureaucrats to be either surly, suspicious, or outraged. In fact they're quite pleasant. Two men, both Chinese—one I'd guess is in his mid-thirties, the other older, perhaps in his sixties. They invite us to sit, they offer tea, they beam when

I say hello in Mandarin, when Zangmo outlines our travel itinerary in the regional Tibetan dialect.

A list of rules, written out in Chinese, Tibetan, English, French, and German is posted prominently on the wall above the older man's desk. They read like commandments, hinting at a richly medieval sensibility and bristling with inquisitorial threat: DO NOT ATTEMPT TO CARRY RITUAL OBJECTS OF ANY KIND OUT OF THE COUNTRY. DO NOT DISTRIBUTE OR DISPLAY PHOTOGRAPHS OF THE SELF-STYLED LEADER OF THE GOVERNMENT IN EXILE, WHICH DOES NOT EXIST. DO NOT SPEAK THE NAME OF THIS PERSON OR ATTEMPT TO CONGREGATE ON HIS BEHALF. RECOGNITION OF REINCARNATED INDIVIDUALS IS STRICTLY FORBIDDEN.

The rules posted in government offices back home seem woefully tame by contrast: IF YOU ARE RENEWING YOUR DRIVER'S LICENSE, FOLLOW THE GREEN LINE. TO OPEN A NEW CLAIM, FILL OUT A DECLARATION FORM AND WAIT FOR YOUR NAME TO BE CALLED. FOR UNEMPLOYMENT INFORMATION AND APPLICATIONS, PLEASE PROCEED TO WINDOW NINE. Our rules limit the direction and activity of the body; our anxieties revolve around property. We're afraid of blocked intersections, illegible forms, spit pooling in the wells of drinking fountains.

By contrast, the rules in the Yushu Tourist Bureau limit imagination, a more flexible and dangerous organ of activity than the body. Imagination can change shape unexpectedly, bend laws, turn back time, fly across borders. Perception, not property, is the chief concern implied by the list of edicts posted here. A peculiar bit of irony that affirms the brand of mysticism the list of commandments seeks to deny.

Time starts to play tricks in Yushu, stretching slowly over a windless afternoon, abruptly snapping together with unexpected purpose: a trip to the Local Government Administration Office, an official banquet, a run for bottled water. It's not certain when we're leaving for Nangchen, where we'll be spending most of our time. "Tomorrow definitely," Lama says; then he adds, "Maybe the day after."

Is his vacillation circumstantial or strategic? Buddhist folklore is full of stories in which teachers test their disciples—commanding them to jump from rooftops, summoning demons, appearing in the guise of lepers, and so on. The aim being to undermine attachments to fixed ideas of what is real and not real, true and false. An untraining of mental habits, not meant to deny the operation of conventional reality so much as to expose its conceptual nature. A rose is a rose is a rose in name only, since it's actually a composite of individual petals, leaves, stamens, pistils, stems, thorns, etc., each of which is made up of various smaller bits of matter, which can be broken down into smaller and smaller particles until the tools for analysis are no longer powerful enough to see the constituent parts. At which point more sophisticated tools have to be invented, which invariably disclose smaller constituents. And on and on.

According to the Buddha, any logical or rational quest for *prima materia* is limited by names and concepts. The goal can only be reached through direct, intuitive experience, the final leap for all mystics, Buddhist and non-Buddhist. Wasn't it Thomas Aquinas who saw something in the chalice during mass and refused to write another word thereafter?

Then again, Lama's hesitation may have a simply practical purpose. People stream in through the courtyard: friends, neighbors, supplicants looking for a blessing for their crops, their sheep, their children. Also sick people who've heard about the American doctor. Kathye sees these people in my bedroom, which by day is transformed into a clinic. The patients are mostly women, some with infants and small children dressed in one-piece jumpsuits that have wide slits between the legs so they can shit and piss wherever without having to be changed or wiped. The Tibetan alternative to Pampers.

Lama and Zangmo translate the patients' symptoms for Kathye then relay her diagnosis back to the patient. The most common problem is arthritis, which sets in early here, as does osteoporosis. Women in their late thirties are already starting to hunch over; by fifty they plod along the hills like inverted *L*s, their spines almost parallel to the ground. Doses of ibuprofen and aspirin are doled out in small paper envelopes, with instructions written in Tibetan: Take two pills in the morning and two pills at night.

There are more serious issues as well: bacterial infections, high blood pressure, goiters, cancer, a number of cases of heart pain. These are especially difficult to diagnose. I watch Kathye listening for irregular beats, checking blood pressure, reading other signs, only to shake her head and declare the heart healthy and strong. The actual problem is recognized only after the arrival of Kunga Nyima, the translator hired to work with Kathye for the summer. Kunga Nyima is a twenty-two-year-old student at the University of Xining, preternaturally shy, sitting on one of the rug-covered planks in my room while Kathye interviews him. He has slightly bulging eyes and black hair worn long, almost to his shoulders. Small hands, tiny feet. He holds a battered, black leather briefcase self-protectively on his knees. The briefcase holds everything he's packed for the trip, which consists mostly of dictionaries: Tibetan, English, a handbook of Chinese medical terms. There does not seem to be much room for anything else.

During the next day's clinic, he solves the mystery of the common complaint of heart pain. A matter of cultural translation. Tibetans locate the activity of thinking in the heart, and the conventional word for heart is the same as the word for mind. So the patients who complain of heart pain don't have angina or clogged arteries. They're suffering from depression.

This comes as a surprise, mostly because it's so obvious: an occupied country, executions, torture, imprisonment; not to mention the widespread poverty, the quotidian hardship of farming and herding, the lack of infrastructure. I've never been more aware of the gift of paved roads, running water, electricity. So many things I take for granted: supermarkets, Band-Aids, cough syrup.

Sitting on the balcony one afternoon sorting medical supplies into plastic bags, we start a communal list of the things we're grateful for.

"Automatic coffeemakers," Jill says.

"Self-cleaning ovens."

We're wearing hats and sunblock. Wisps of dust swirl in the empty courtyard below. Lama and Zangmo have gone off somewhere with Jampay. Where is unclear. Martha sits washing socks and T-shirts in a metal basin painted with flowers. The hot water comes from a thermos. It's the same water we use for tea. The basin is what we use for sponge baths in the morning and at the end of the day. Shampoo doubles as laundry soap, so there's one less thing to carry. Or leak.

"I actually like it," she says. "The simplicity. It's refreshing not to have to think about those things."

She'd cut her hair just before we left the States. Now it's short, barely covering her ears, exposing her neck. The style emphasizes the Americanness of her face, the slightly dazed quality, confident, oblique. Eyes and mouth a little wide, smallish nose. Polymorphic origins. She blushes easily.

"I don't know why we call them conveniences. They're not convenient. You have to clean them, cart them around when you move."

"Lint brushes," Kathye says.

"And who's going to fix them when they break?"

I'm seated cross-legged on the concrete with three piles in front of me: analgesics, vitamins, and unsorted items. My left leg is on the verge of falling asleep. The trick is to figure out how to move it without messing up my piles.

"Coupons," I say.

"Grapefruit."

The point of the exercise, we decided at the outset, is to name things that aren't obvious, but which contribute in some profound way to one's sense of well-being.

"Oh, my God," Jill says, "cappuccino."

"What are these?"

Kathye leans over to study the bag of pills I've plucked from my unsorted pile.

"Decongestants. Chockful of tiny time capsules for sustained delivery of antihistamines. Blue suitcase."

All the supplies donated by various pharmaceutical companies and hospitals—the tongue depressors, assorted bandages, the strips of individually packaged disinfectant towelettes—are randomly mingled among several boxes and suitcases. Cotton swabs. Antibacterial

ointments. Jars of B-complex vitamins. The virtues of
organization have become apparent after just two days
of seeing patients in Yushu. Ten or fifteen minutes to
find a bottle of amoxicillin is too long. So we use our
downtime to sort: vitamins and analgesics in one suitcase, cough and flu remedies in another, antibiotics and
other prescription medication in another.

"And these? Why do we have a whole box of salad
tongs?"

Kathye, Jill, and Martha are silent.

"Those would be vaginal speculums," Kathye finally
says, "For gynecological exams."

She takes the box and puts it in the miscellaneous
suitcase, along with the trial-size bottles of mouthwash
and the box of rectal thermometers.

"I don't know why we have those."

At night, in bed, I continue adding to the list: salad bars,
American Express, vending machines. I find it hard to
sleep in Yushu. At first I thought it was the noise—another surprise. I'd expected to find in Tibet the kind of
nighttime silence one finds in the country, loaded and
intricate, the susurrating distraction of insect chatter, animal laments. Instead, around eleven or twelve, the dogs
around the city start howling. First one dog, then another, followed by an eruption of canine voices that continues more or less unabated till dawn. No one can
explain why; it's just a feature of the Tibetan night, like

the stars, the colossal silhouettes of the mountains guarding the horizon.

Magazines. Multiplex theaters. Scotch tape.

Neither asleep nor awake on my plank, sleeping bag pulled up to my neck against the cold night air, winter coat rolled up as a pillow beneath my head.

Deodorant.

Thumbtacks.

A viscous, blue-black light saturates the room, a film of oil across the lens of night, through which certain objects manage to articulate their presence. The small, round loaves of bread on the table by my bed. The aluminum thermos near the door. Scattered on the plank beneath the window, my cassette tapes of spoken Tibetan, which I've carried halfway around the world but have yet to listen to, their smooth plastic cases enchanting a stray shaft of moonlight.

And the goddamn dogs.

It's so clear, the contest between my will and the noise outside. And clearly ludicrous, since the battle exists in my imagination only. The dogs are going to bark, regardless; I want them to stop, regardless. For a good half hour longer the conflict between these two extremes continues. And then abruptly stops. I don't know why. It's not fatigue or resignation; the battle lines are still are still as clearly drawn. There's simply, momentarily, a framework large enough to include both the noise and my need for it to stop.

I fall asleep, counting the things I'm grateful for instead of sheep.

Flatware. Cordless telephones.

E-mail.

These are the landmarks, the topography of experience I take for granted. Identifying them point by point this way feels like meeting someone for the first time.

All told, we spend five days in Yushu. On the morning we're supposed leave for Nangchen, we wake to armored skies and a torrent that churns the courtyard to a muddy pond. It's said that great lamas, by their very presence, conjure rain: a gift of fertility, restoration of the land, a mythic healing—thrilling to witness though inconvenient when planning a road trip.

"Must leave five A.M.," Lama had insisted the night before. Kagi had already gone ahead in a truck loaded with the medical supplies and the larger of our suitcases.

Rain hurls itself in against the windows, passionately, a deeply committed rain. We eat breakfast in my room, Kathye, Jill, Zangmo, and I, in somewhat awed and subdued silence. Canvas shades have been unrolled outside the windows in an effort to keep water from blowing in through cracks in the windowpanes, imperfect seals. A naked, ten-watt bulb suspended from the ceiling of my room makes a heroic effort to illumine the five-foot-square area directly underneath. We sip tea from the camp mugs we brought with us; we spread jelly of indeterminate color and origin on round loaves of *balop*. We're wearing coats and thick sweaters. Absent direct sunlight, the temperature has dropped precipitously because of the rain.

Kunga Nyima, our translator, is still too shy to join us in anything but an official capacity. He prefers the company of Jampay and Rigdzin. At night he sleeps in Jampay's jeep. Jampay occupies the front seat; Kunga Nyima sleeps in back. Rigdzin sleeps in his own jeep. Since we've taken over the rooms on the second floor, the rest of Jampay's family—his mother and sister, his niece and son—share two makeshift bedrooms on the ground floor.

Martha has not joined us either this morning. She's still in bed, suffering an extreme bout of food poisoning.

"I think she'll be okay," Zangmo says, in a tone remarkable for its lack of conviction.

Jill scrutinizes a piece of *balop* for signs of mold or itinerant insect life. "You know, I thought that meat looked suspicious."

"It was stomach," I remind them.

Kathye stirs a spoonful of dried cranberries into her instant oatmeal. A seasoned traveler through challenging places—Vietnam, Saudi Arabia, Thailand, India—she has packed her supplies insightfully. "Stomach is meat."

"In a broad sense," I argue. "A categorical sense,

which would include any number of unsavory items. Eyes, for instance. Toes. Organs of excretion."

"All perfectly acceptable forms of vitamins and protein. You're just being petty."

"Definitely ethnocentric," Jill says.

The indirect cause of Martha's illness had been a banquet held the previous afternoon, hosted by several county-level administrators. We'd had to dress formally: an uncomfortable project in itself since we'd had no opportunity for more than a daily sponge bath since leaving Xining. It's not a happy feeling, putting on a suit and tie when your skin is crusty with dirt, dried sweat.

The site chosen for our banquet, a restaurant on the main street of Yushu, exuded the grim, dispirited pall of a Nevada truck stop bathroom. Traces of biliary green were still evident on the concrete walls, but the paint was for the most part faded and chipped; a thick film of something, grease possibly, formed a kind of dull glaze overall. A paper calendar hung on one side of the room, a picture of a marginally forested gorge along the top, the individual squares representing days of the month marked with Chinese numbers.

A ratty yellow cloth had been strung across the entrance to the area where we were seated in an effort to protect the privacy of the local officials and their esteemed guests. Unfortunately, no similar precaution had been taken to prevent passersby from stopping and gaping at us through the large window overlooking our table. An unnerving experience, looking up to see three or four ragged figures pressed to the window glass watching you eat.

Several brave souls even ventured inside, pushing past the yellow curtain to confront us more directly. One was a tall, reedy monk, using his knit cap as a begging bowl while he chanted prayers at us. There was also an old woman, either weeping or pretending to weep, moans of agony leaking from her toothless mouth. The restaurant proprietors rushed in, grabbed the beggars by the elbow, and hustled them out; then returned bowing, grinning, begging our forgiveness for the interruption. There was something almost zany in the repetition of the scenario, a madcap, Ernst Lubitsch quality. With very little effort of imagination the scene could have tipped from tragedy to farce.

There was also the food. Steaming bowls of inchoate lumps caught in a kind of gelid petroleum. Deep-fried lumps. Lumps on skewers. Lumps arranged in concentric circles on a plate, sprinkled with sugar. Lumps that secreted a greasy amber venom. Lumps masquerading as egg rolls, as noodles floating in pallid sauce, as dumplings, fried or merely boiled.

I hewed as closely as courtesy allowed to a menu of Pepsi and rice. Martha, the most adventurous among us, tasted everything. Dishes a starving cat would decline. We made occasional attempts to dissuade her from a few of the more noxious-looking entrees, but there was a thrilling aspect to her experimentation, a recklessness in which we all to some degree participated.

"How many times did she throw up last night?" I ask Zangmo.

"Four. Five."

"And how many times did she . . . ?"

"I think she only went down once, but she stayed a long time."

I feel compelled to catalogue the particulars of Martha's illness. A warding gesture. Also an assertion of faith in the determinative power of details.

"We won't be able to leave today."

Zangmo shrugs, smiles. "I wouldn't be too sure."

"There's a deluge outside. Our photographer has a severe case of food poisoning."

"Must leave five A.M.," Kathye says.

"Or not," Jill replies.

"Or not. The first time I was in Vietnam I was told that I was going to be picked up at nine in the morning for a funeral. I got dressed in what I considered an appropriately somber outfit, lightweight, but funereal. I waited with my hosts in front of the house where I was staying. At two o'clock we were picked up and taken to a wedding."

"But there's a welcoming ceremony for Lama," Zangmo says. "Just outside of Korche. The children from the satellite school there."

"Zangmo, this is the kind of weather that makes people start drawing plans for an ark."

She laughs, not with me, but at me. At my fixation on the obvious, as potent as superstition.

"I don't think that matters," she says.

Lama opens his door suddenly and addresses Zangmo, half in English, half in Tibetan. His tone is brusque, almost impatient. Zangmo replies that she thinks whatever he's looking for may be in one of the bags in her room. She gets up, wraps herself in her coat, and hurries out. A burst of mud-scented cold blows through the room and sets the naked lightbulb swinging. A muscular, raw wind, long-fingered, inquisitive.

Moments later Lama comes out of his room wearing a jacket and knitted cap, deep red, both of them, wool. We stand automatically, out of respect, and he laughs— chuckles, actually, in response. An acknowledgment charged with multiple significances: happiness, amusement, chagrin. A layered response in the face of which it's hard to maintain any self-congratulatory attitude toward one's own sense of having done the correct thing, the pious thing.

As Lama heads for the door, we follow like anxious ducklings, quacking and gabbling about the rain, the cold, the wind, reaching for umbrellas, plastic bags, hats—something to shield him and, incidentally, ourselves—from the elements. And again he laughs, heading out onto the balcony, down the ladder.

We follow in turn and assemble on the front porch, slightly damp but curious. Zangmo descends a few minutes later carrying a small brass chalice and a tarnished teapot. Jampay's sister brings out a pan of hot water and fills the teapot, then throws in a handful of dark twigs, Tibetan tea. Rain slashes the courtyard. Lama waits for the tea to steep.

A woman wails, high-pitched, a radio voice.

Puddles overflow into tiny, interconnecting streams, and a perfect topography of muddy islands and embankments takes shape, small, shifting continents. The sky is the color of old ashes. The house exhales mildew.

At first Lama's voice is nearly indistinguishable from the rain. A gravelly murmur, threading syllables through the regular splash and patter of water falling on mud, on walls. Zangmo fills the small brass chalice with tea and passes it to Lama. He holds it up, like a toast, hurls the contents out into the storm, and passes the chalice back to Zangmo. She fills it again, passes it to Lama, who toasts the storm again and pours the tea into the wind. The offering is repeated several times. Lama continues chanting throughout. Then he stops.

"Okay," he says.

We file into the sitting room and watch Chinese folk singers on the television. The singers are mostly women, dressed in long gowns with dramatic, flaring sleeves. They wander among gently sloping hills, across fields of swaying grass, sometimes pausing by a tree or the bank of a river, cantillating happily and diatonically about, presumably, the glories of nature. Sometimes a young man in uniform appears on the scene as well, energetically praising wheat, or cherry blossoms, rice. They seem to inhabit an orderly, wholesome world, these singers, free from heartbreak and jealousy, irony, loneliness. They radiate confidence, a contentment with things exactly as they are.

An hour later the rain stops.

The road is a broad, pulpy gash winding erratically across an undulating field of spongy green. Mud regularly halts our progress. Tires spin, axles sink. Rigdzin and Jampay rock their jeeps back and forth to ease them out of the deeper and more glutinous puddles.

An attempt to bypass the road altogether and drive directly on the turf ends in middling failure. The terrain is studded with rocks and sinkholes, and spectacular bumps frequently jog loose whatever has been crammed in the narrow space between the backseat and the trunk: boxes, knapsacks, bags of rice. They sail forward, sometimes narrowly missing our heads, sometimes connecting. It's after we crest an especially rocky patch and nearly tip over that Jampay gives up and returns to the road. Rigdzin, behind us, follows suit. I'm not sure how long I've been clutching the edge of my seat. My knuckles are white, my fingers stiff and bloodless.

There's some consolation in seeing Zangmo flex her

fingers as I do, and catching the same vestiges of anxiety and horror on her face.

"You could look at this," she says, "as an opportunity to deepen your understanding of impermanence."

"How funny you should say so. That's exactly what I was doing."

"I could tell."

"I was radiating serenity, wasn't I?"

"Glowing."

From the front seat, Lama wants to know what we're talking about. Zangmo leans forward just in time to avoid being grazed by a sleeping bag jolted loose by another bump.

"We were just saying," she explains, "what a perfect opportunity this is to practice." There's a suggestion of irony in her voice. Of the self-deprecating, not the caustic, variety.

"Excellent driving," Lama replies.

His tone is neutral, and it's impossible to determine what he means by the remark.

It only becomes clear how high we've climbed when we stop for lunch; although the elevation is not the first thing we notice. First, everyone sploshes rather hastily through the mud in different directions, seeking a hollow or crevice. Everyone except Martha, that is, who remains in the front seat of the second jeep, knocked out by a dose of Halcion to get her through the worst of the trip, which is difficult enough without food poisoning.

I clamber, half sliding, down a small hill. The land-scape is virtually featureless: not a tree, not a shrub, only a tiny stream, trickling half-heartedly across a rocky bed. I tell myself I will get used to this, the squatting, the adjustments required to avoid an embarrassing accident. I will develop strong thighs, an acute sense of balance. I will be a fundamentally saner person. The things I tell myself to get through a challenging situation.

Once we reconvene around the jeeps, Zangmo extracts a paper bag full of *balop* from the backseat; Jampay lo-cates a thermos of hot water. A jar of jelly is found and a small package of Laughing Cow cheese that one of the nuns back in the States had thoughtfully packed. A plas-tic bag of Tetley tea. Strips of dried yak. The idea of lunch occurs spontaneously, collectively.

We carry our makeshift picnic to an outcropping of rock, the driest spot in the vicinity. We use camp knives to spread glistening orange marmalade on the flat rounds of *balop*, steep tea in the heavy aluminum mugs we've bought in sporting goods stores back home. Despite the extreme conditions endured during the past three weeks of travel, the Laughing Cow cheese shows no signs of spoilage, a convincing testament to the virtues of proc-essed food.

"After the bomb," Jill predicts, "there will still be Laughing Cow cheese."

"Spam, too, I would hazard to guess," Kathye says.

"I'm sure the cockroaches will be pleased."

The sky has shifted from gray to white. With the sun reasserting itself directly ahead, it's warm enough to take off our jackets, though we keep our sweaters on. From where we're sitting, it's easy to see how the road we've been traveling on slopes gradually downward. It vanishes into an almost gelatinous patch of fog, reappears in the distance, then vanishes again into the mist.

"I suspect those are clouds," Kathye says. "We're above the cloud line."

Jill asks Zangmo what our elevation is. Zangmo, in turn, asks Lama how high up we are.

"Twelve thousand feet," he says, then confers briefly with Jampay in Tibetan. He turns to Jill. "Fourteen thousand."

"What does that translate to in terms of miles?"

A panel-stumping question.

"Three," I hazard.

"Or is it four?" Zangmo asks.

"Three miles."

"Or four."

"Hallucinations are not uncommon at this elevation," Kathye says. "Headaches. Shortness of breath. It would be a good idea to avoid overexertion."

"I guess that means we scrap the aerobics class today."

"Not a bad plan, all things considered."

Jampay and Kunga Nyima get up from the circle and

move away to smoke. Rigdzin opens the hood of his jeep and pokes among the wires and tubes, tinkering, adjusting. Slowly we pack up the lunch things, shake the tea from our mugs.

How small we are under the open sky, cleaning our hands and faces with antiseptic towelettes: not a tree for miles; dark green hills on all sides rising and falling like a primal ululation of the earth itself; below, the tops of distant mountains poke through gray lakes of cloud. The road ahead is lost to the horizon.

We brush the mud and crumbs from our clothes and return to the jeeps, a company of pilgrims.

"It's not much farther," Zangmo says.

Three hours later, we're still driving. It's easier going though. The roads are drier, and there are fewer stones and sinkholes. Shacks appear on the sides of the road, single-story huts of mud brick with vacant windows and curtained doors, shapeless laundry hanging limply along lines of nylon rope. A scene of archetypal desolation. Dirty-faced children with wise and terrible expressions; adults plodding down the streets in ragged clothes and the eyes of agonized innocence.

After another half hour we reach the gates of a Gelug monastery, the name lost in the sudden rush of sensory details: buildings of various sizes, in various stages of construction, dogs barking, rows of mud brick drying in the sun. Men with wheelbarrows scuttling back and forth. Monks in the main courtyard stare, not overtly hostile, but not welcoming. It's a complex scene, thick with heat and dust, shades of suspicion. Until the Chinese invasion, the Gelug order had been the dominant political power in Tibet for nearly three hundred years, but their control over the eastern kingdoms was always tenuous.

An older monk approaches, heading quickly from around a building to the right. He smiles as he greets Lama, and then we're walking up a broad flight of steps, along a veranda, leaving Jampay and Rigdzin behind to watch the jeeps. Hardly a burden, at least for Rigdzin, who has already pulled open the hood of his vehicle and begun poking around the engine. I can't help but wonder what he finds so compelling there.

We arrive, ultimately, at the quarters of a bald, aged lama, the director of the monastery: a paneled room with a wood floor, chairs and benches draped with hand-woven rugs worn to a sheen. Attendants bring in cups and pots of milky tea, along with a plate of packaged cookies and another of hard candies. The conversation flows animatedly between Lama and our host. And I realize that one of the things that distinguishes them from the younger monks outside is that they belong to the time before the invasions and revolutions. Before imprisonment, exile, the burning of monasteries. Before the flight to the West and the return. The environment they

grew up in was radically different in ways I cannot com-
prehend. And they're alive at the other end of the process. They are the last of the Mohicans.

Though I can't tell what they're saying, the rapport
between them is curiously reminiscent. I'm reminded of
Sunday afternoon visits with my grandmother, when she
would call on her sisters or cousins, old neighbors,
friends from childhood. They would speak in Italian—
the language of their childhood—of a shared time now
lost. A language in which to speak of dramas, people,
and times unfit for the ears of children. A language of
secrets, which gives rise in me to the same emotions of
exclusion and also of privilege. It's like watching a sacred
mystery unfold: a world, a history, and eventness so close
I can almost touch it. But only almost.

I've discovered in this room the religion of my youth.

When we leave the monastery, Zangmo tells us confi-
dently that it really won't be much longer now before
we reach Korche.

"Or not," Kathye says.

Zangmo laughs. "I remembered it being closer. I'm
sorry."

Jill parodies a squint. "I don't know. Should we trust
her this time?"

"I don't see that you have much choice."

Half an hour later it starts to rain again, a sporadic

drizzle. We're also climbing again. The angle of our ascent is steeper; ropy clouds slue past the jeep windows. Rain turns the tundra a deep, almost ruddy green.

The jeep skids and bounces like a small boat on rough seas. Sometimes all four tires lift off the road at once. Once we almost tumble over the side of a cliff. I can safely say that prior to that moment I had never ridden at a forty-degree angle to a precipice.

Zangmo's face, when I regain enough composure to turn my head, is the color of damp paper.

"I'd always heard that facing death at close range is supposed to make one feel more alive."

"That's what they say," she replies. Hoarsely.

"I'm not so sure I agree." I can feel the blood gradually returning to my extremities. "My personal response, in fact, is much more bunny in the headlights than stalwart game hunter."

Zangmo tests the possibility of smiling. "I think that's what the Bardo is supposed to be like."

I have to digest this a moment.

"You mean that was a clear light experience?"

"I think so."

"A revelation of the nature of mind, completely illumined type of experience?"

"Could be."

"And I missed it?"

"No, you were there. You were just paralyzed with fear."

"But isn't there supposed to be bliss? Divine song? Rainbows? A spontaneous rain of flowers?"

Zangmo presses her lips together, shakes her head sadly. "It's supposedly pretty devastating, actually."

This, too, needs digesting.

"Well, then, what's the point?"

"The point is if you can recognize the experience as the essence of your own mind, then you're free."

"Free from what?"

The jeep hits a particularly egregious bump, and a bag of bread sails between our heads. I catch it one-handed before it reaches the front seat.

"From," Zangmo continues, after momentary reflection, "the suffering that arises from clinging to the idea of a having a definite self."

"That sounds like something you read."

"It *is* something I read. It's also what the masters of the lineage have described as the truth."

Confirmation of some sort is required, so I lean forward and ask, "Lama, a few minutes ago when we nearly rolled over the cliff . . . ?"

"Yes?" he replies, turning very slightly toward me.

"Zangmo says that was a clear light experience."

"Oh, sure," he says. Pleasantly, jovially.

"And I missed it because I was too scared."

"Sure, sure," he replies.

I lean back, half-consciously extracting a piece of *balop*

from the bag and starting to nibble on it. Jampay says something to Lama, and Lama replies at some length. Then they both laugh. I assume, self-centerdly, they're laughing about me. Which feels a bit like almost rolling over a cliff.

The rain comes and goes. We bump along a muddy strip of road though dark swaths of tundra kissed by roiling clouds. We scuttle past mountains veering toward us like hungry ghosts. We cross another plateau, climb another pass. Another three hours go by.

Then we're rounding a bend and suddenly: people. A ragged handful, damp, dressed in military jackets, torn blazers, muddy boots. They seem almost to have erupted from the ground, emanations of the earth, a bit wild-eyed, luminously grinning. Gorgeous and slightly terrifying.

Jampay pulls to a stop, and the small crowd collects around Lama's side of the jeep, ducking their heads in turn as he reaches out to bless them and then drapes shorts lengths of red yarn, protection cords, across their necks. One and then another glances curiously at the tall bundles in the back. It's almost funny to see the shock register as they distinguish us, pallid and slightly worse for wear, but the genuine article all right. Westerners. They press close to the windows, pointing and staring.

Now Jampay is inching the jeep forward. A pair of boys splits off from the crowd to run ahead, wanting to be the first to announce our arrival, but there hardly seems a need. Already people are surging down the road toward us; and from over the hills, horses, draped in multicolored silks, hooves pounding a frenzied rhythm, fanning out on either side of our two jeeps; the men on their backs shouting, waving banners. We weave slowly through dense clouds of blue-white smoke spilling from stone altars, banks of waving, cheering people, and come to a stop finally about twenty yards from a makeshift arch: two tall wooden posts topped by a long wooden beam, wrapped in a garland of juniper branches. Monks in ceremonial robes of yellow and gold sound eighteen-foot horns to the accompaniment of giant drums and heavy cymbals. A thundering, joyful cacophony that literally shakes the earth.

As Lama emerges from the jeep, the crowd presses forward, people sinking to their knees, prostrating themselves on the damp ground, reaching forward to touch the hem of his robe, his shoes, his hand. He touches their bowed heads, their shoulders, their outstretched hands. Ties protection cords around their necks. A monk appears beside him holding up sackful of hard candies, which Lama distributes to the children, the aged. At the same time, amid the thickening altar smoke and the clattering music, a pair of wiry monks lead a saddled horse toward the jeep and help Lama to mount, while four others—carrying an enormous canopy of white, red, and yellow silk—assume positions on either side. As Lama settles on the back of the horse, the horns and drums, if possible, ratchet higher, louder. Men in costume— dressed as demons, as yak and horses, a snow lion even, as terrifying deities bound to protect the Buddha's teachings—scramble through the crowd to the head of the procession, which staggers slowly, noisily through the juniper-draped arch into the courtyard of Korche monastery.

Once through the arch, Lama dismounts and leads the way toward a large, three-story building that occupies the center of the monastic complex: the *lha kang*, the house of divinities, the temple. Lama rounds the corner to a side door and enters, surrounded by the senior monks of the community. Following, we enter a dark, stone vestibule. Shoes are hastily kicked off, people file into the main hall: a massive, gloomy cavern with a packed-earth floor and walls hung with painted scrolls showing various aspects of the Buddha and other sacred images.

In the far corner, a tiered shrine burns with countless butter lamps, the light fractured and reflected on the sides and surfaces of metal bowls filled with saffron water. A strong, sweaty scent of yak butter fills the hall. Long, low wooden platforms are arranged in rows perpendicular to the tall, painted throne where Lama has been seated. Monks and other honored guests—ourselves included—sit on the platforms; the rest find places on the floor facing the throne or behind the platforms. A line of monks proceed up the center aisle to make the ritual offerings prescribed for the arrival of an important lama. The entire scene is lit somewhat luridly by a trio of naked bulbs powered by a small, gas-powered generator. Which fails two-thirds of the way through the ceremony, leaving us to the dim flames of the butter lamps.

At the end of the ceremony, after the main crowd disperses, we follow Lama and a handful of monks through a door at the back of the main hall into a long, narrow room: windowless, low-roofed, almost a cave, dominated by a massive, gilded statue of the Buddha. Lamps and candles surround the statue, generating a soft yellow glow. Lama hangs a *kata* on a thin cord stretched in front of the statue. Here there is profound silence.

In the vestibule outside the main hall, a stone staircase ascends steeply into darkness. Monks holding flashlights lead Lama and our small party up to the second story, our shadows playing gaudily on the damp stone walls. We arrive in a long, broad room with a dais at one end set up for Lama and a bench along the left side for us; the resident monks of Korche—dressed now in their ordinary robes of dark red cotton—arrange themselves in rows on the dirt floor. Most of them are young men in their early twenties and thirties. The few elderly monks sit closest to Lama; one is his uncle, Tenzin, who managed to keep his monastic commitments even during the worst years of the occupation. Another is an old man with a long nose and a rough, gray beard; a knuckle-sized cyst protrudes above his left eyebrow.

Dusky light filters through leaded windows set at eye level in the walls. Night collects itself in furrowed clouds, darkening the view of distant mountains, the trampled mud of the courtyard below. Huge pots of boiled rice are carried in, along with bowls full of heavy strips of boiled yak, wooden pails of acrid yogurt, jugs of Tibetan tea, soupy greens. A tray of dry, sand-colored cookies sprinkled with hard candies wrapped in cellophane. A short blessing is chanted, which gives way to the husky murmur of conversation between Lama and the monastic residents, a susurrant growl punctuated by the smacking of lips, the grinding of teeth against tough meat and gristle. The darkness intensifies, encapsulating the thick smells of damp clothes, damp earth, unwashed bodies. Boiled meat.

Soon all we can see are the eyes of our hosts, the dim outlines of their robes.

"We left Yushu exactly fourteen hours ago," Jill says.

ELEVEN

A foreign queen in an untamed land.

She misses some things. Floors, for one, the sturdiness of marble; cool tile beneath her feet. A sense of propriety for another, a certain delicacy in the way of speaking and gesturing, sitting and standing, inconspicuous but telling. Here her subjects watch her openly, as though she were a curiosity too extreme to ignore. Not just the women, but the men, too: the ministers and advisors, the supplicants; the plotters against the king of this unruly nation, her husband. Against herself, too, probably. She is, after all, a foreigner, her dowry a foreign message—*fo jiao*, the message of Lord Buddha. The native priests distrust her. They sit in rows on carpets thrown over packed earth, staring, muttering to each other, their lumpen frames swaying under heavy robes, showing pale gums and the brown stumps of decaying teeth.

For a long time she'd thought they were muttering about her, but she's learned enough of the language to know they're only going on about their children, their servants, the encouraging glance the king, her husband, gave to this one, the frown he showed to that one. She herself, the embroidery, the ceremonial serving of tea, the concentration with which she works at translating a book from the language of the Middle Kingdom to the language of this barbarian outpost, carefully tracing gold ink onto silk died the color of the sky in summer: These serve merely as an occasionally interesting distraction. She could be a bird, a dark cloud passing slowly overhead. She could be a goat. But she is a queen, the wife of Songstengampo, a holy king, the first of this wild nation to recognize the value of the *fo jiao*. The first to seek the holy teachings for his people. A rain of blessing will fall on this land.

Fresh fruit. She misses that, too. What she would give for an orange, a ripe pear. A plum. The last messenger her father sent from China had brought silkworms, swords, a book on astrology, a medical book, and a dictionary. Along with the usual flourishes and praises, polite inquiries on the health of his daughter, congratulatory remarks on her husband's conquest of some province to the west. A crate of salted fish. Pigments for the temples being built around Ot'ang, the little lake in the middle of the capital whose name she still has trouble pronouncing: Xra-sa, Ra-sa, Xla, Sa.

No plums though.

And not a single orange.

To be expected, of course. A second daughter of a second wife of an emperor can't expect to be remembered personally. She wonders if her father even recalls her name, if he ever really even knew it, the T'ang emperor: a man capable of killing his brother and forcing his own father to abdicate. She'd only seen him twice, at a great distance. Once at the deathbed of the dowager empress, his mother, and again when she was presented to the ambassador her husband had sent to acquire her.

She silently tastes the sound of the name her new people have given her, the arch of the tongue against the roof of her mouth. Unshing Kongjo. The tartness of the vowels.

I will never go to such an evil place.

Stories had come East about Tibet: demons, ogres, dragons in the water, a freezing desert where nothing grew and the mountains gleamed like white fangs. Like all things, partly true. There are places north of Xra-sa where the air is so thin and dry that snow does not fall in winter. And some of the old women do look like ogres, humpbacked, cackling, one eye smeared with milky white. The men paint their faces red when they go to war. The local magicians offer blood, the carcasses of dogs and cattle, to make the rain come and go, to make the crops grow, to stop a flood. They fling horns filled with gold dust at their enemies to cause sickness and famine. They hallucinate unruly manifestations with six arms and matted hair, dressed in tiger skins and ornaments of skull and bone: spirits of rocks and waters; unquiet ghosts of forgotten ancestors troubling a village, the entrance to a pass, fouling a river, drying a well. The sincerity of what they see, of the incantations they recite, their mystic formulas of balance and appeasement. She feels foolish sometimes, not believing, too, not seeing, only tolerating their stories with a nod and a half smile.

It is a land of famines, a race of ogres, flesh-eating demons: if I must go to such a place.

Not to mention the sheer expanse. Nothing at home in Chang'an could have prepared her. The journey west to Xra-sa, where the king had made his capital, had in itself lasted six months, over mountains like the broken forms of fallen giants, gray bones showing where the green had been scoured away by wind, by rain, the white sun. After weeks of traveling, no cities, no place you could call a town, no encampment even or watchtower, you could believe: This valley is the bend of a massive knee, this sluggish river an artery pulsing with slow life. You could describe patterns, discern subtle shifts in temperature, the thickness of the air, the condition of the soil. You could develop a rapport with the deep, raw life of this place—the horizonless steppes, the vaulting sky— a reverence for it, a love, even.

And then they come.

A trickle at first, singly, then in pairs and trios, in their filthy coats of black wool, scraped leather, their fur caps. Lice wriggling in their greasy hair. The broad faces, the wonder. Bearing gifts: a tiny, carved deer, a plate of chipped stone, a twisted lump of metal said to have fallen from the sky. Amber. A square of clean cloth. Roasted barley ground to a coarse flour, *tsampa*, which is mixed with butter and hot water and eaten, raw, as dough. They walk beside her caravan for miles, sometimes days, weeks, then slink off in the night—her new people.

She asks the Tibetan ambassador, mGar, *What is this name they call me?*

It's after lunch, and the entire company is sprawled on the dry yellow grass beside a stream. A broad, silk parasol has been erected to shade her from the sun, hung with long strips of yellow, blue, white, green, embroidered with gold thread. A throne draped in silk is set on thick wool carpets, the whir of crickets. Laughter, far off, and the noise of water; the clang of kettles being washed out by servants.

Drolma, liberator.

The ambassador says it is the name of the patron goddess of his country, who was born from a tear falling from the eye of the Compassionate, All-Seeing Buddha, Chenrezig. Then he tells the story of how in the last Iron Ox year, the Buddha of Compassion had looked on his country, the Land of Snows, and saw the time was ripe for the people here to learn the profound truth spoken by the Awakened One, the Lord Buddha, in the holy land of India. Four shafts of light then erupted from the body of the Compassionate One. From his heart, light filled the womb of the Tibetan queen, Driza Tokarma, who gave birth to Songtsengampo, the current king. A birth marked by signs, rainbows, flowers cascading from the sky. The earth shook six times. The infant bore the imprint of the wheel of truth on his palms and the soles of his feet. The Buddha of Limitless Light sat upon his head.

The drone of bees, the blue smoke of juniper laid on cooking fires. The ambassador's secretaries, the guards, listen respectfully. Her women, fans fluttering softly, the papery wings of moths.

Light from the right eye of the Compassionate One reached the country of Nepal and entered the womb of the consort of King Amshuvarrnan, who gave birth to an exalted princess with white skin tinged with red: Her breath was the purest sandalwood incense, she was skilled in all fields of learning, the Princess Tritsun, the elder queen of King Songtsengampo. To the Land of Snows she brought a golden idol of the Buddha of Unshakeable Essence.

From the mouth of the Compassionate One, a stream of light poured down into the center of the Land of Snows, and the six-syllables of liberation spontaneously appeared in the stones of the Yamtrang Precipice: *Om Mani Padme Hum.*

The guards murmur the holy syllables, the secretaries, the cooks, even the nomads who have joined them, voices lapping, a series of waves rippling outward, flattening the dry grasses, stilling the water.

Om Mani Padme Hum.

A fish leaps, flash of sunlight on silvery scales. Birds wheel overhead.

And the fourth ray? She asks this.

If I must go to such a place.

From the left eye of the Compassionate Buddha, a shaft of light stretched toward the Middle Kingdom, to the valley of Chang'an, the palace of the Emperor T'ai Tsung, and entered the womb of his consort, who gave birth to an exalted princess versed in all fields of knowledge, with skin tinged blue, breath the scent of a blue lotus, a fragrant body circled ceaselessly by a turquoise honey bee. Her right cheek was marked with the spots of the divine dice, her left with the imprint of a lotus. On her forehead was the image of Drolma, protectress of the Land of Snows. She was born to be the younger queen of Songstengampo, bringing with her from the Middle Kingdom an immense golden statue of the Buddha—created during his own lifetime and blessed by the Awakened One himself—the mere sight of which has the power to dissolve ignorance and illumine the minds of those who seek the truth.

He tells her this, soberly, plainly—though she has no marks of any kind on her face and her skin isn't blue.

Though she is afraid of bees, turquoise or otherwise.

Her ladies, behind their fans, show nothing.

Though her breath, especially in the morning, does not smell of lotuses.

She does, however, bring the statue, a concession from her father to the foreign king turned to the words of the Awakened One. Suddenly she decides to build a temple for the gift she brings, gilded, the walls exquisitely painted with scenes of the life of the Buddha. There must be a grand pageant with flutes and bells, thick clouds of burning sandalwood. Drums. Torches. Suddenly, such plans.

The people will love her.

Such plans.

She is a girl of thirteen.

If I must go to such a place.

She will tame demons. She will bring peace.

A rain of blessing in the palm of her hand. There is a certain satisfaction in a missionary venture. In bringing hope and healing to a benighted nation. She is blessed.

The people will love her.

TWELVE

And the rains come: not the harrowing torrent that had delayed our departure from Yushu, but a chill, intermittent drizzle that insinuates itself into socks and sneakers, the folds of clothing—an inescapable dampness.

We're lodged in a two-story house roughly perpendicular to the west wall of the *lha kang*. The lower floor is reserved for dry storage, which consists mostly of bales of hay, fifty-pound bags of rice, and long, broad stacks of yak dung, the only viable source of fuel here above the timberline. The odor is a challenge surpassed only by the clouds of ripely scented smoke that occasionally roil into our rooms from the kitchen, when the cook—a short, hunched woman with black braids, apple-doll skin, and obsidian eyes—forgets to open the flue of the dung-burning stove.

Our rooms are on the second story, reached by a ladder placed at a nearly perfect right angle to the lip of the hole cut in the floor of the second-story hallway. The hole is large enough to eliminate the risk of hitting my head, but the steep climb is surprisingly exhausting. At fourteen thousand feet, even minimal exertion leaves me breathless.

At the far left end of the hall is a room where Tenzin, Lama's uncle, lives. His personal shrine is there, set with small statues of the Buddha, several butter lamps, and seven bowls of saffron-scented water, each symbolizing a specific offering to the Buddhas: water for drinking, water for washing the feet, flowers, incense, scented water, food, and music. The room also holds a three-foot-square wooden box with a tall, wooden back where Tenzin sleeps at night, sitting upright in a cross-legged meditative posture. The practice of sleeping upright is undertaken formally during the traditional three-year retreat, during which the core teachings of the Kagyu lineage are transmitted and, through months of intensely focused practice, internalized.

A door to the right of Tenzin's room opens into our living area, which consists of a somewhat long, narrow anteroom with mud brick walls. The only light comes from a kerosene lantern suspended from a ceiling beam. Plank benches line the walls, about two feet high, each draped with a scrofulous-looking Oriental rug. The dirt floor has been churned to thick mud by the crowd of monks and villagers who have come for an audience with Lama.

At each end of the room is a door to a small bedroom. Zangmo and Martha share the room on the left, which contains, in place of plank benches, two actual beds; a degree of luxury offset somewhat by the presence of a red-lacquered cabinet that contains a small chest full of *tsampa* and a large burlap bag filled with yak butter.

The opposite door leads to Lama's room, which also has a bed, piled high with thick carpets and blankets, and a floor of unfinished wood. While Zangmo settles herself and Martha—who is sleeping soundly after another dose of Halcion—in their room, Kathye and Jill choose two of the plank benches in the anteroom and start unrolling their sleeping bags and pulling various supplies from their suitcases. I sit in bleary limbo on the remaining bench, wondering where I'm going to be billeted.

I don't have to wait long for the answer. After several minutes of bustling activity in Lama's room, Kagi emerges and beckons me closer. I see the bed, the wooden floor, Lama conversing with his uncle and several other monks; however, I don't see any likely place for me to sleep. Then Kagi points proudly to a pile of oily rags on the floor.

From a traditional Buddhist perspective, of course, sharing a room with a lama is an extraordinary blessing, irrespective of the quality of the bedding provided. I know I should accept the honor with delight. But to-night, with the rain, the disastrous jeep drive, the cere-monies, and the long interval of dinner, it's a struggle to choose between the possibility of beatitude and the cer-tainty of discomfort. In the end my solidly middle-class conditioning wins out, and I beg Zangmo to explain to Kagi that I prefer to sleep in the anteroom with Jill and Kathye on the unclaimed plank bench.

The kitchen adjoins our living quarters. It's a dolorous little cave dominated by a pale, misshapen lump, which on closer inspection turns out to be a stove made of concrete. Food is prepared on a wooden table littered with bits of meat and other, indeterminate matter: barley, maybe rice, vegetable scraps.

At the far end of the hall is a wooden door that opens—astonishingly—onto an indoor bathroom the size of a largish coffin. No light, no window. The small hole in the floor leads directly to an open pit in the ground below. A certain amount of dexterity is required to undo one's trousers, hold onto the flashlight and avoid dropping the toilet paper, while navigating into a posi-tion that maximizes accuracy and minimizes strain. Af-terward, heading back down the cramped, dark hallway to our rooms feels like navigating a catacomb.

As the evening progresses, the features of this place we've landed in begin to coalesce: the mud, the dirt floors, the densely poignant odor of unwashed bodies and dirty clothes, the silent, dark-eyed monks sitting in neat rows watching us unpack, wash our faces in a basin of hot water, burrow into our sleeping bags. Through the windows in our room, a glimpse of moonlight, preternaturally bright, pierces the heavy clouds. A lone dog paces the courtyard outside, wailing.

It's past midnight when the last visitors leave and Kagi extinguishes the lantern in our room. His footsteps recede down the ladder, out the front door. With darkness comes clarity: that our journey thus far has encompassed a distance not merely geographical, but temporal. We've staggered back a thousand years. The few exceptions— an unreliable electric lightbulb, the haphazard modern clothing—accentuate the stubborn ancientness of these mountains, these drafty rooms, the scarecrow nomads, their faces lit with hope and awe. History is rooted here, a howling pageant of tribal kings, warring clans, religious ecstasies, armed invaders sweeping down on horseback, the ineradicable reek of atrocity, blood, charred bones. It's an anguished presence, not hostile, not warm. It waits, though for what is hard to say.

The days pass in fits and stretches. At dawn the horns and drums of morning prayer shake us out of sleep, and the tinkling of small cymbals announces that Lama and Zangmo are performing *chu tor*, a ritual offering of food and drink to the suffering spirits of the lower realms. Kagi enters with thermoses of hot water and then again with a bag of *tsampa* and a wooden bowl of yak butter. Lama emerges from his room, and we share a makeshift breakfast: tea, *tsampa* mixed with nuts and raisins, instant oatmeal. There are no plates or spoons; we use the small bowls, travel mugs, and camp utensils we'd brought with us, washing them after each meal with tepid thermos water and a drop of shampoo.

Despite the rain, people come to see the American doctor: men and women, children, fifty or sixty everyday. Where they come from is a mystery as I see only one house near the monastery: a crumbling waddle-and-daub cottage with a roof of dirty thatch. They straggle out of the mountains in groups of three and four, in their damp clothes, hair plastered by rain, hobbling down the road like wounded ghosts, veterans of a forgotten war.

A makeshift clinic is set up under a roofed, L-shaped portico that adjoins the *lha kang*. Medical supplies are laid out along a set of wide, concrete steps that line the short leg of the portico. Jill, Martha, and I take turns locating the required medications, wrapping them in small envelopes of brown paper, and passing them down to Kathye, who sits cross-legged on a rug at the bottom of the steps, patiently measuring blood pressure, assessing the rhythms of Tibetan hearts. Kunga Nyima kneels at her side, navigating between the medical tomes Kathye has given him and his dictionaries of Chinese and Tibetan language, translating symptoms and diagnoses: arthritis, pneumonia, hypertension. One or two possible cases of tuberculosis. A surprising number of goiters.

"There's no iodine in the salt," Kathye mutters, scribbling kelp tablets on her list of supplies to bring next year. "No seafood in their diet."

Surprising, too, is the way the young and healthy shove past their elders for a chance to be examined. The first morning threatens to collapse into chaos before Kagi and several other monks, at Kathye's request, herd the eager crowd into something of a line. Urgent cases first, then women with babies and children, followed by the aged, the crippled, cases of lingering disease. After lunch, a curtain of faded cotton cloth is hung in front of the examination area to discourage spectators—knots of young men mostly, slouching under their rain-soaked fedoras, smoking cigarettes, laughing. For them the clinics are a form of entertainment, a novelty inserted into an empty round of days spent loitering, watching animals graze, throwing stones at dogs.

Children run around the courtyard, screeching, playing hide and seek among the small, whitewashed houses behind the *lha kang* where the monks live. Adults congregate in groups under the eaves of the nearby monastery kitchen, a long, low building ruled by a short, cross-eyed monk with long, crusted nails and a mouthful of rotting teeth.

The elderly take shelter where they can beneath the roofed portico. They sit twirling their prayer wheels, a type of religious implement that consists of an axle and a rotating brass cylinder lined with long, thin strips of paper. The paper is scribbled thousands of times over with the mantra *Om Mani Padme Hum;* and as the cylinder spins, the power in the sacred syllables is diffused in all directions to invoke the blessings of the Compassionate One, Chenrezig.

"Old bones," Kathye tells a woman in her early forties, already twisted with arthritis. "Wrap warm rags around your hands to make them feel better. Your wrists and elbows, too. Your knees. Lie on your stomach with a warm rag across your hips."

She demonstrates while Kunga Nyima translates, pausing while he looks up the Tibetan word for "elbow," "hips." On the steps above, I twist a square of brown paper into an envelope and Jill drops in a dozen tabs of ibuprofen.

An enormous yak slowly crosses the courtyard.

A group of monks file into the *lha kang* for afternoon prayers.

An old woman hobbles from the portico to shit in the grass. The young men in their fedoras watch her, laughing.

These are our days.

When I'm not helping out in the clinic, I visit the *lha kang*. It's not a comfortable place: It's cold and dark, lit only by the butter lamps on the shrine and by a few slitlike windows close to the ceiling. The stone floor is crusted with old mud and dried gobs of phlegm randomly spit by a number of the monks during group prayers. The air is thick with the heavy smells of mildew and yak butter and the hemplike aroma of Tibetan incense. An atmosphere at odds with the luminous, vaulting intimations of holiness to which Western churches aspire. A different order of sanctity permeates this place, a sacredness that admits of earth and blood and horror, the sheer catastrophe of human life.

This disturbing gestalt is the legacy of monks and scholars of eighth-century India, gifted men shattered by a holistic vision that burst like lightning in the middle of an otherwise ordinary afternoon. Raving, they fled the austere comfort of their monasteries to wander graveyards, haunted forests, cremation grounds, engaging fear directly, the terror of death, annihilation; and like the Buddha before them, they saw through the monstrous, mesmerizing, perishable *I* to realize what they always were: uncreated, undying. Empty.

Thus was born the Vajrayana, which, ferried across the mountains by Padmasambhava, found its perfect setting in the fierce and lonely landscape of Tibet.

Sometimes, sitting in the *lha kang,* the presence of the early masters is palpable, a desolate current, half-threatening. I'm a pious fraud, chanting prayers in a language I don't understand. Then a group of monks file in for evening prayers. Surprised by my presence, the younger ones crowd around, leaning over my shoulder to see what I'm reading. Their soft noises of recognition and approval. Tonight, I'm chanting prayers to Tara—Drolma, in Tibetan—the female Buddha who manifests twenty-one different forms to overcome the various obstacles to enlightenment. A beautiful but very complicated visualization to maintain, even without a group of young Tibetans hovering.

The Master of the Chant clears his throat, and the novices hurry to their seats. Once they're settled, group prayers begin: a rhythmic, atonal chant, punctuated by bells, horns, the baritone throb a giant drum, and occasionally a loud, hawking expectoration.

Our arrival at Korche has coincided with the end of the monastery's summer retreat—or *yarnay*—an intense period of study and reflection on the core texts of the Buddhist canon. The *yarnay* tradition is actually quite ancient, dating back to the time of the Buddha, who regularly retired with his monks to various donated settlements during India's summer monsoon season. In Tibet the tradition is embellished with a three-day festival to celebrate the conclusion of the retreat.

Despite the chill wind and iron clouds that mark the first day of the festival, a brave caravansary of the faithful can be seen coming down the road: young women in long, wool skirts, their hair dressed with lumps of coral, turquoise, and amber, or braided with colored ribbons. Fathers cradling brightly dressed children in their arms. The swaggering young men, drinking from flasks. Ancient women all in black, hobbling along, spinning prayer wheels as long as their arms. Most are walking, a journey of several miles for some, but there are also men on horseback, monks rakishly straddling motor scooters, a procession of ancient, battered jeeps.

The end of their journey is a high plateau behind the monastery where an enormous white canopy has been erected. Lama and the monastery's senior teachers sit on thrones set up along one edge of the canopy; the rest of the monks settle in rows on the ground. At a signal from Lama, a young monk standing just outside the canopy begins slowly beating a handheld gong, inviting the buddhas, bodhisattvas, protectors of the Dharma, and local gods to join the celebration.

In fact the first two hours of the festival consist of an offering ceremony to these spiritual entities. A large, roughly circular fire pit has been dug a few yards from the canopy; and at intervals throughout the long chant, a procession of monks heads toward the flames carrying platters of food—yak meat, yogurt, butter, rice, barley, and large bowls of tea and barley beer. The food is thrown directly onto the flames, while the monks who carry tea and beer circumambulate the fire pit, flinging the contents of their bowls toward the sky. The flames leap, crackling; twisting beards of acrid smoke climb toward the sky.

The circling, the offering of meat and grain, it's hard to resist the mimetic power of these ritual gestures, the sprinkling of consecrated liquid on holy ground. Even the young men are silenced. Even the children succumb to the spell of patterned memories reaching out from the deep past.

Abruptly, the chanting breaks off. And then resumes. A momentary cessation, a gap in which it seems the world's rotation stops and time and eternity briefly, gently, touch. It's so full, this fleeting interval of meditative silence, an offering more pleasing and more profound than all the food and drink—in receipt of which the local gods perform a miracle, splitting the clouds with a thin, transparent rainbow.

The climax of the *yarnay* festival is an opera, performed by elaborately costumed monks in a large, open area in front of the canopy. It's a meticulously choreographed event, every step and gesture performed according to a plan laid out centuries ago by someone whose name, whose place of origin, are lost. But the pattern remains: chaste, methodical, achingly serene. The monks perform without singing, acting out the story while the score is scratched out on a battered cassette deck, a pantomime with music, disembodied voices floating tremulously under a bright summer sky.

The plot comes from the Jataka tales, an ancient set

of fables, chiseled, polished by generations of nameless village poets; blind grandfathers passing on their sparse inheritance of moral wisdom; mothers soothing restless children through the gathered monotony of the summer rains. No one knows who collected them or what Southeast Asian Homer performed the final synthesis, transforming the entire canon—five hundred stories of wise elephants, greedy crocodiles, and benevolent kings—into a grand, metaphysical epic that describes the gradual spiritual development of the Buddha over the course of five hundred incarnations. A kind of alchemy, this fusing of separate sparks into one jewel.

The opera that unfolds, gravely, slowly, under the white Tibetan sun is the story of Vessantara, prince of a mythic Indian kingdom. At age sixteen he marries a beautiful princess, played by a rather grumpy-looking young monk weighed down by an enormous headdress of feathers and plastic flowers. Naturally generous, Vessantara ends up giving away the entire royal treasury to his subjects, which enrages his parents, the king and queen, as well as the royal ministers. The prince is sent into exile with his grumpy wife and their two children, played by two of the youngest novices. A slow half-circle around the playing area marks their unhappy journey into a dark forest, where the impoverished family live together in a decrepit hut.

One day, while his wife is out gathering firewood, Vessantara meets a greedy old Brahmin priest, who asks the prince to give him his two children. Without hesitation, Vessantara agrees, and the novice monks are tied with vines and led away into a life of slavery. Later, another Brahmin approaches the prince and asks for his wife; and again, without hesitation, Vessantara complies. After a third Brahmin demands that the prince give him his eyes, Vessantara stumbles blindly through the forest until he reaches his father's kingdom, where the Brahmins are revealed as gods whose terrible demands were meant to test the depth of Vessantara's generosity. The prince's sight is restored, along with his wife and children; and in a stylized dance of joy, the king and queen reward him with the gift of the entire kingdom.

I find the story appalling. What kind of man would sell his children, make a whore of his wife, and plunge his kingdom into chaos—all for the sake of an ideal? Could it really be generous to cause so much suffering? But when I glance over at Lama, I see the tears running down his face. And I have to ask: "Why are you crying?"

Eyes brimming, he turns to me. "I'll never be able to achieve such commitment."

I don't know what to say, how to respond to this intensely personal confession of failure. An honor, but also a burden I'm not sure I'm fit to receive. I still cling to a host of ordinary attachments—to friends, family, a desire for success in the world. Even the desire for enlightenment, according to the Buddhist scriptures, is attachment, which must be overcome: the taint of expectation, of hope, reinforcing an idea of missing what you already have.

My mouth is dry, my stomach hurts. I could believe it's just the lunch of stale cookies and warm Pepsi. Or parasites breeding in my guts. A virus. Anything but the fear of being asked to give up something I don't want to lose. Anything but failure.

Late in the afternoon, after the opera is over, a group of nuns arrive, a journey of almost a hundred miles from their monastery in the south of Nangchen. Kneeling before Lama, they tearfully beg him to visit them in the convent he built for them in the shadow of the Kala mountains.

Over dinner, he announces that tomorrow we will ride to the convent of Kala Rongo. And while the prospect of another grim jeep ride through the mountains doesn't exactly thrill, I can't deny a certain quivering excitement. Greedy anticipation. In the Kala mountains, high above the convent, is the cave I've traveled ten thousand miles to see.

THIRTEEN

We'd planned to leave Korche by eight, but a group of people had walked out of the mountains in the early morning mist to see Lama; and after the interview, he asked Kathye to examine them. One, a man of fifty or so, with strawlike gray hair, was diagnosed with old bones. His wife—or mother, it was hard to tell—had high blood pressure. The younger couple were apparently healthy; but to compensate them for their long journey, Kathye gave them each a packet of six multivitamin tabs. It was after eleven by the time they left.

"Hmm, must leave at eight," Kathye said, packing up her stethoscope and blood pressure cuff.

"Or not," Jill replied.

Kagi shepherded several of the novices upstairs to carry our luggage down the ladder and out to the jeeps.

Then we were off: Lama, Kagi, Zangmo, and I in one vehicle; Kathye, Jill, Martha, and Kunga Nyima in the other. We were descending now, climbing down the other side of the mountain range that sheltered Korche.

We hadn't gone half an hour before a man standing on the side of the road waved us to stop. He prostrated to Lama, then urged us to follow him a few yards down the embankment to a flat spot where he'd set out a picnic of yogurt, dried yak, and bread. I wouldn't have minded the yogurt, but couldn't get beyond the fact that it was stored in a converted gas can. I ate bread and watched the ground quiver with grasshoppers, thousands of them, copulating under the polished sky, the burning sun. It felt good to be outside in fine weather.

After twenty minutes we returned to the jeeps and continued down the mountains. Our route took us through a deep gorge, its walls curving inward like massive ribs. The sun vanished; primeval dusk prevailed. Partway through, a stream swollen with a week's worth of rain had spilled over onto the road. With a mighty effort, Jampay's jeep made it through the sucking mud, but Rigdzin's was caught. Every time he pressed the gas pedal, the axles shrieked like wounded animals. Kagi and I paced back through the muck to help Kunga Nyima push the jeep through. Our feet sank; clots of mud spattered our clothes, our faces, which made us laugh. When the jeep finally shot forward, it seemed as if the ecstatic, ringing noise we made had convinced the muddy road to release its hostage.

They saw us coming down the road: the students, the teachers, the local government officials, converging on our jeeps as we pulled to a stop. A joyous frenzy partly inspired by the fact that we were four hours late. The children chattering and singing, trailing the long sleeves of the folk costumes they wore; the adults grinning and bowing, shaking hands. Clouds of red dust enveloped us as we walked down the path to the schoolyard.

The main school building faced the Mekong River, a broad, green, rippling dragon. We sat on a stone patio shaded by a broad swag of red cloth as the children fanned across the dirt courtyard and began to sing, reedy soprano voices rocking up and down a chromatic scale. They danced as they sang, twisting their sleeves like streamers, red, yellow, blue, under a white sun. Afterward they lined up to receive the gifts Lama had brought over from the States. School supplies, mostly donated. Notebooks, pens, pencils. Crayons. Scissors. A few toys. Then we filed into a classroom to hear them recite their lessons, the entire group reading aloud from Tibetan texts. A shattering cacophony but also magnificent, considering the impediments of place and fate that stood in their way.

The children were dismissed, and we followed our hosts into a smaller classroom where tables had been arranged in a horseshoe shape. Flies swarmed over the food laid out for us, a familiar offering of dried yak, yogurt, bread, washed down with Pepsi, Jian-Li Bao, or brackish tea. Several of the local officials rose to make speeches, thanking Lama, their new American friends, the kind people whose donations helped the poor children of Tibet. I dreamed of salads. A breeze broke through the windows, fanning our paper napkins and setting the flies in motion. We ate cookies that tasted exactly like sand. On opposite walls the masters of the Kagyu lineage gazed benignly on framed photographs of Lenin, Stalin, and Mao Tse-tung.

After lunch, the officials departed. We returned to our jeeps and drove across a concrete bridge that spanned the Mekong and ended in front of a shattered mountain.

Nobody told us the road had been blown up. A curious omission, since it was the only route to Kala Rongo.

"A construction project," Zangmo says, translating the information provided by the man beside her, a school official of some sort, Tibetan, but dressed in a Chinese military jacket and cap.

He waves his knobby fingers at the gray slope of shattered rock ahead, then turns and points back behind us, across the bridge we've stopped on, beyond the school, on the other side of the river. Yes, there's a road there, if you squint, a sinuous brown line looping away south and east toward Shornda, the district capital. Our informant waves his hand now, as if directing the stones over the water.

"They're going to pave the road over there," Zangmo explains, pointing across the river. "So they blew up this road to use the rocks."

He might be fifty, the school official, or he might be thirty. A sense of accelerated wear bears down on him, a phenomenon I've noticed during the three weeks we've traveled in Tibet: the sudden descent of age like a winter nightfall. The young wear their beauty effortlessly, their glossy black hair, dazzling teeth, skin like polished wood. At about the age of twenty-five, their teeth begin to loosen, elbows pop, arthritis warps the hands. Is it the altitude, I wonder, or the weary round of scraping barley from hard soil, coaxing livestock out to graze and back again? Or boredom, the endless work of repair, molding bricks from straw and mud, patching shoes, whittling a tent stake from a chunk of horse bone adventitiously discovered in a field?

The school official wears a soiled T-shirt beneath his military coat, and drawstring pants the color of dry mud. The big toe pokes out of his left shoe, like a joke, a sly grin. His orphan apparel makes him look young, belies the knobby hands and missing teeth.

"They'll take the rocks from here," Zangmo says, when he has finished speaking, "and haul them across the bridge to the other road."

A fold of her robe flaps wanly in the limp breeze that crosses the bridge where we're standing. Other members of our party have moved closer to the rubble to examine the project: Lama, Jampay, Rigdzin, Kagi—and Notra, one of the Korche monks. Also three nuns from Kala Rongo, girls in their twenties, with broad, grinning faces and short-cropped black hair. Lama and Jampay are talking with the laborers.

"Notice they're all Chinese," Jill says, behind oversized dark glasses and a rumpled canvas hat, protection against the sun. "No Tibetans."

"Transplants," Kathye says. She's leaning against the cement rail of the bridge, shading herself under the cat-eared umbrella she'd bought in Beijing. "Bring in settlers, give them the high-paying jobs. It keeps the native populace depressed."

"Drugs are good, too. They work."

"Not to mention blankets infected with smallpox."

Zangmo asks a question in Tibetan, leaning closer to the school official to catch his response.

"Oh, oh, oh," she says, nodding.

It turns out to be the bluff overlooking the road that was blown up, not the road itself. The rocks will be carted away and pounded to gravel or used to buttress the edge of the Shornda road, which extends a little too precipitously in places over the Mekong River. What remains of the cliff stares, red and raw, over the detritus at its base. A sense of catastrophe hovers around the stones: imminent tragedy on a scale that mocks our civility, our jeeps, the bridge, the thin plastic water bottle we pass among ourselves to clear the dust from our throats.

Tibetans won't work on the project, the school official tells Zangmo. Three people have died since work began. The first, a foreman, had a sudden heart attack. The second, also a foreman, was struck by lightning. A third man slipped while climbing across the rocks and fell half a mile to the river below.

There's awe in his expression as he watches Zangmo relay these details to us. And another emotion peculiar, fierce. There's a god in the mountain who is understandably outraged at the desecration of his abode; retribution will be taken. The fierce emotion in the official's face is joy.

We work our way slowly, hand over hand, across the rubble, parallel to the cliff face. Testing each unstable stone with our toes before resting our full weight on it. I don't know whether to ignore the steep plunge down to the river below or to will myself to focus on the peril. Either way, the even chance of dying here is an immovable condition, larger than myself. What I think about it is, by comparison, chaff.

Behind us, students from the school pick their way lightly cross the stones, carrying our luggage. The three nuns who met us at the school haul huge sacks of rice, their *jowlas* slung over their shoulders crammed with vegetables, candles, other goods they'd bought in Shornda, a distance of thirty miles at least. I wonder if they'd walked all the way there. Maybe not: along the roads through Kham, we've sometimes passed flatbed trucks with hitchhikers crammed in the back, an assortment of red-robed monastics, workers, nomad herders. They always wave when we pass, grinning, sending shouts of greeting cartwheeling past us to tumble across the broad, blank tundra where they dissolve and fade, mingling with the elements, a polyphonic chant reverberating in the giddy splash of summer rain.

The temptation is to read a kind of innocence in their shouts and waving, a simplicity: riding in the open air, the community of fellow travelers; a confidence in the sure, nimble steps of schoolchildren across loose rubble; in the bright, insouciant chatter of girlish nuns. Except that here, now, hugging the unstable stones is neither simplicity nor innocence. Without thinking I set my foot on a loose rock and slip, pelted by an avalanche of sharp pebbles, scrambling for purchase. Shrill, shocked cries tear the air around me, now above me, as I slide, fall, dive backward with unintended grace over the river rising to grip me in its cold, green hands and drag me under, chased by an exhalation of disbelief and the splatter of loose stones. A vivid experience that would be: precise, direct, but not simple, not innocent.

The far end of the cliff face curves back from the river and gradually melts toward a narrow dirt road. A few yards farther from where we touch, gratefully, solid ground is a flatbed truck parked backward with the cab pointing at the road ahead. Jill, Kathye, Martha, and I pitch ourselves up into the back, while Lama and Zangmo take seats in the front. The brigade of children, monks, and nuns who follow hand up our luggage. The children wave good-bye; the three nuns, along with Jampay, Kunga Nyima, Kagi, and Notra, clamber up into the back of the truck with us. In the driver's seat, Rigdzin starts the engine, a rapturous growl like a bear shaking off its winter sleep, and the truck huffs and shudders down the steeply descending road.

Sitting is a test of will. Cracked stones pock the road, each one a jolt that shocks my spine. The boxes of medical supplies, the sacks of rice, slide precipitously back and forth. A tomato pops out of a bag and rolls, zigzagging, the entire length of the truck bed. The truck tilts sometimes at perilously acute angles to the road. After five minutes I can't sit anymore.

I follow Notra's example, stepping to the front of the truck bed, buttressing my legs against a pile of suitcases, and grasping the vertical metal bars that separate us from the cab of the truck. Notra grins at me. He's tall for a Tibetan, standing nearly five foot ten, his height accentuated by the *sham tab* and long-waisted coat he wears, both of which he made himself out of light wool dyed a brighter red than one usually sees. Almost scarlet. As is his wide-brimmed hat, which he also made. He has a thin, black moustache and wears aviator sunglasses. "The coolest monk in Nangchen," Zangmo calls him.

Notra is an artist; more precisely, a painter of *thankas*, icons painted on silk scrolls. Working out of a tiny, mud-floored studio a few miles from Korche, he uses pigments made of crushed minerals, water, and glue, and brushes tipped with mountain lion fur. Delicate work, exquisitely detailed. The figures must be drawn precisely, according to rules established hundreds of years ago and handed down secretly from master to pupil. Sacred formulas that invite and contain the being or force depicted in the *thanka*. After days of working ten, twelve hours without pause, Notra has told me, he suffers crushing headaches, blind spells of anxiety and depression, an agonized withdrawal from the fevered presence of gods and monsters.

Right now, he's jubilant, nodding, drawing my attention to the crumpled green mountains across the valley through which we're hurtling at death-defying speed. Here, the river is yellow-gold. White clouds swim like whales through a liquid sky. I want to photograph the scenes as they speed by, to fix them, hoard them; but I can't let go of the metal bars. We're plunging and climbing so fast my hands ache with the pressure of holding on, careening over rocks with such force that all four wheels bound off the road at once. Beauty and terror rise together in the same bright, painful flash of apprehension.

We climb a hill so steep it seems impossible not to roll back down, a violation of natural law. Halfway up, the jagged tips of distant mountains pierce the sky. As we reach the crest, Notra smiles, points straight ahead toward whitewashed buildings that rise in tiers against three sheared mountains, gently tilting toward one another other like massive flatirons. In single file a procession of nuns winds down a narrow ledge of road to greet us with horns and cymbals. The slow beat of a massive gong fills the air. Rising from stone altars on the side of the road, thick clouds of juniper smoke turn copper in the first rays of the setting sun.

"Kala Rongo," Notra says.

I don't believe him. I think we must have died at some point along the perilous road. We've fed on lotus petals, drunk the milk of paradise, pierced the veil between two worlds. A gust of wind will shred the scene.

The truck stops; we jump down onto solid ground. The nuns surround us, real enough, draping *katas* over our necks. Real enough, the laughter of the younger nuns, the brown-toothed smiles of the old ones. We pace slowly up the narrow road in the cool shadow of the mountains. The cave waits, above, somewhere.

After Korche, Kala Rongo is a miracle of cleanliness and order. Our rooms, on the second story of the *lha kang*, all have wood floors, swept and washed daily by the nuns. Electric bulbs hang in every room, powered by a large gas generator; the lights come on at dusk and go out punctually at ten o'clock each night. Only the dining area recalls antiquity, with its dirt floors, the slab of meat crawling with flies that hangs from a post in the middle of the room.

But if time crawled at Korche and in Yushu, here it flies. Days pass in a dizzying progression of ceremonies, interviews, clinics, picnics of tea and cookies in the surrounding hills. Occasions insert themselves, allowing us to catch up to ourselves. One night the nuns gather in the *lha kang* to perform the ritual of *Chöd,* a mesmerizing, lyrical chant accompanied by bells and handheld drums.

There's a trip to Shornda, back across the rubble, into the jeeps parked at the school, and ten miles along a road clogged with construction machinery, a journey of three hours to a town of baked mud roads lined with spindly trunks of long-dead trees: tethered yaks awaiting slaughter, a field lined with billiard tables, an open-air market piled with wilting lettuce and wrinkled, green tomatoes. Crowds of boys and men follow us down the main street, awed by the abrupt appearance of Westerners in their midst. They follow us inside cramped dark shops, pressing close to pull the hair on my forearms, an almost fearsome prodigy compared to their bare brown limbs—though no less shattering than Kathye's blonde hair, Martha's close-cropped shock of red. Or Jill, a woman wearing pants. Their eyes batter us; their fingers probe; warm breath pours down our necks.

Two days after Shornda we make a voyage through

the mountains to an open field, a sprawled mud-thatch
house fenced with low, stone walls. From all directions
a slow gathering of nomads come to see the doctor. A
groaning woman crawls on hands and knees to the blanket where Kathye sits with Kunga Nyima, assessing
symptoms, prescribing treatment. Boys pelt grazing yaks
with stones. Young mothers rock malnourished babies in
the shadow of a stone wall. Men collect in groups, smoking, laughing. The sun burns our skin.

Every few days I venture some question about the cave:
How high is it? Among so many openings and crevices in
the mountain face, which is the special one? Lama's answers vary. It takes a half a day to reach, the route is tricky,
maybe a few of the younger nuns should guide us. Maybe
we should take horses: a plan which, in fact, emerges in
our final days at Khala Rongo, when Lama announces
over breakfast that when we leave the cloister and return
to Korche, we'll go on horseback, taking a route up and
behind the mountains. Rigdzin and Jampay will take our
luggage in the truck by the ordinary way through the
valley, over the stones, to the school, where they'll pick
up the jeeps and drive to Korche.

On the day of our departure, the nuns gather in front
of the *lha kang* with their bells and hand drums to perform the ritual of *Chöd*, wrapping a spell of benediction
around us as we head up into the mountains. Their

voices follow our ascent, riding the air, tattered rhythms of an ancient song.

The sun shines hard on the slopes, picking out details: the tough, spiked leaves of springy ground cover, imprints of our horses' hooves, a scattering of yellow flowers. Lama rides in front with Kagi and Notra; the rest of us fan out behind—Kathye, Jill, Martha, Kunga Nyima, Zangmo, plus a group of three or four men from a village hidden somewhere in the folded hills, our guides and protectors. They've supplied the horses and will lead them back after we reach Korche.

We ride under a vaulted sky, clear and empty. For the first time it hits me that in all the days we've spent in Tibet, I haven't seen a single bird, just the void above, blue or thick with rain, or black, cut with unfamiliar stars. Nights are haunted by the noise of howling dogs; days, by the sound of human voices, the clatter, roar, and pounding of tools fashioned out of wood or stone or metal. How this place endures without softness, sentiment, a lyrical nostalgia to cushion the inexorable mundane round of grief and loss and change is a mystery. I'd turn away, but the mystery remains. A riddle: What you see is what you see you see.

We ride higher, tracing the curve of the mountain until we're behind it. Lama dismounts and the rest of us follow suit to spare the horses through the next part of the journey, a long, rocky ascent up the back side of the Kala mountains. By the time we reach the end of the path, I'm puffing and sweating, but the view astonishes: a broad plain of sparkling green, gently sloping, sheltered by the Kala mountains on one side, a lesser range on the other. The plain ends abruptly in a steep drop. We sit on the edge, staring down on the Mekong as it winds through a narrow defile between two mountains.

Pointing to a crevice in the mountain wall across the river, Lama says, "That's where I went after finishing my second three-year retreat: six months, meditating, practicing. And there," he twists around and gestures back toward the rolling slope behind us, "is where the Communists came through my country. I watch them come over the hill: an army, a thousand men, two thousand. They go down; they burn the villages; they kill all the animals, the people. I hear the shooting clearly. I see the monastery burning clearly.

"And I wait—two months, three months—for winter, for the river to freeze. Then I come down at night and walk across the river, and walk: two hundred miles, three hundred, four hundred. To India is very far."

A breeze rustles his robes.

"But you were caught, weren't you, Lama?" Zangmo asks.

"Oh, sure, sure," he replies off-handedly, an old story.

"How did you get out?" This is Jill.

"My lama. He comes one night while I'm sleeping and says get ready. He comes the next night and says get ready. The next night and the next night, same thing.

He's dead three months already but still comes. Then one night he says go. What can I do? He's my lama, very good lama, must do what he says, must go."

"And nobody saw you?" I ask.

He shrugs. The question has no meaning.

"Not the guards; not the other prisoners?"

Lama shifts his legs, turns slightly, pointing right toward a set of hills. "My cousins lived there, my aunt. They were so crazy"—he laughs, squinting, eyes like crescent moons—"but good people, kind people." Inhaling deeply, sighing out. "All this land was theirs."

The breeze blows; below, the river follows its course.

"Okay," Lama says, "must go now."

Rooted, I watch them slowly pace the field: Lama, Notra, Kagi. Red figures in a field of green. The others follow behind. Something starts to slip, opportunity, passing, about to pass. I want to be an astronaut. I want to fly through space. I want to melt past prison guards in the dark of night.

Too late, I think, but running anyway. A cloud skids across the sun. And when I catch up to Lama on the rocky trail, heading down now, away from the mountains, I can hear the plaintive dullness in my voice. Having made the journey, but missed the point. Asking, "What about the cave, Lama? When do we see the cave?"

FOURTEEN

Where did he go? the old king wonders, sitting erect on
the stone floor of his room. Rumors came and went,
stories of spontaneous healing, demons rounded up and
tamed, cataracts released from solid rock to water farmlands burned by drought. He would be quite old now,
his master; even a man miraculously born from a lotus
flower would feel the weight of age, the anxiety of bones
wanting final rest.

I'm finished here. I will go among your people.

And he went: teaching, planting seeds, hiding treasures for generations still unborn. Thirty years ago they'd
built this place together, Samye, a fine monastery, a good
place to retire after handing down the reins of power to
a son thirteen years old, a fragile boy under such a heavy

crown. Still, the traditions must be observed, and he'd had enough of ruling.

To meditate, to contemplate, to feel the winds rush through his body. The lights coursing through his bundled nerves. Peaceably in a stone-floored, stone-walled room, empty save for a wooden shrine, a lamp, metal bowls for offerings. Not even a bed, a chair. After all the pomp and intrigue, the border wars, the endless formal bickering of ministers hostile to a new religion.

Words, words. As a boy, he'd learned the Dharma in secret for fear his ministers would find out. The sudden death of kings is not uncommon, and he had brothers. How easy to carve his name upon a standing stone, Trisongdetsen, boy king, buried with his fathers. Dead now, all of them, the threatening ministers. To outlive those once feared invites a special brand of grief. And peace. Which is, and is not, what he'd expected.

The letter in his lap, from the eastern provinces, says his old master appeared not long ago, sailing on a rainbow in the form of a white deer. He hopes it's true, that the old man is still capable of marvels. Precious Teacher, the people call him now, Guru Rinpoche, hardly what they'd muttered thirty years ago.

And even he must admit that, after months of anxious waiting, hope, the back and forth of coded messages signaling delays, the arrival of the sage from India had failed to impress. A short, old man with green eyes, windchapped face, rags on his back, still limping from a bad case of frostbite. No sacred texts; no ornaments of power. Not even a horse or mule. His only companions are an ugly woman with big teeth and a half-dead disciple who fainted halfway through the ritual of welcome.

Now he can laugh, see the justness in this beggarly approach. But as a young man of twenty, seeking strength, guidance, a helpmeet for his kingdom, he'd felt humiliated. A chalky taste of disappointment had gathered in his mouth.

The Cave

FIFTEEN

Sometimes I'm walking down the street and a wind blows past me hard on its way to somewhere else. This happens quite often in Brooklyn, where I live at present. There's a strip of road between my apartment and the F-line subway stop; a tall, brick school on one side, Prospect Expressway on the other. The wind that sometimes passes down this street varies in quality, gentle or harsh, cold or warm; but always when it comes a stillness follows, a pregnant calm that surrounds the bleating truck horns, the rushing traffic, the noise and color of children whirling down the sidewalk on skates. It lights the living pattern to which each separate element belongs. This wind, I know, has grazed Tibet. Its clarity is familiar: the sting it carries, and the comfort of it.

Why am I a Buddhist? I wonder sometimes, still: about the Dharma, its fierce, light touch. I'd tried so many paths before with the same results. First, a period of blissful equanimity, a relief wrought by looking at the world in a fresh perspective; followed by a rash of personal calamities, tests of faith, trials—the boggy waste of latent thought exposed by prayer and meditation. A long, hard task of cleansing.

In this respect, the Buddhist path differed little from others I tried. The first six months after I took refuge was a period of intense joy, a radical rediscovery of a world I thought I'd grown weary of. It began as a matter of ordinary listening. Words and phrases repeated during seminars, again in the Buddhist literature I read, began to irritate. Flecks of dust in the corner of my eye. Odd images, unfamiliar ideas spontaneously disrupting the constant rhythm of my internal chatter.

For example, Tibetan masters often refer to the individual self as a "stream of being": in the sense that an enormous variety of conditions contribute to the life of every moment. Focus on the breath, sit up straight, keep your eyes open, and sense the multiplicity of phenomena occurring in this instant. Sounds, smells, itches. All of them transient, all rising and falling in a field of awareness that forgot it could also be aware of itself, of its own dimensionless plasticity—just grazing which feels like gaining a new sense organ.

It's possible to fall in love with the idea of the richness of this experience; though life in its sheer transience usually provides sufficient opportunities for disillusionment. A healthy balancing out. A recognition that endings are endings as well as new beginnings, and that what is mourned is only partly what has passed; the other cause for grief is what will never be. Call it hope, call it fantasy, call it reasonable expectation. What is mourned is an idea.

About a year after I became a Buddhist, a long-term relationship had begun to come apart. There had been problems, naturally, over five and a half years, failed connections, disagreements. We didn't notice the vitriol slowly seeping in. The chanted lists of what was going wrong between us, the canticles of one another's faults. My lover didn't favor my new interest in Buddhism, the hours of prayer and meditation, weekend trips to the monastery upstate. "You spend more time banging cymbals and ringing bells than you do with me," he would say. He was right.

Nel mezzo del cammin di nostra vita: the approach of middle age announced itself with confusion, a rattling sense of lost direction, of opportunities receding. Death joined the party in its most revealing mask since my uncle's passing when my friend Neff, diagnosed too late with a tumor, entered Sloan-Kettering. One by one his organs failed. He vanished daily.

His parents came to bring him home to Oklahoma, and my lover and I went to make our final visit over Thanksgiving. We stayed in a motel, a tawdry dark place with a flamingo-colored neon sign, rooms that smelled of camphor and stale cigarette smoke. We spent part of Thanksgiving night at a Big Boy diner on the main street of town.

Neff was on a strong morphine drip; the most either one of us could do when we visited him in his room at home was lay next to him in bed and hold him while he saw things: men with rifles by the window, monsters on the ceiling, devils hiding just behind the door. Horrific visions, burst at times by fits of clarity and confession in which he catalogued his regrets, the women he'd walked out on, the slightly dingy ordinary life in small apartments in New York, lost loves, a failed career in acting. So much he'd wanted to do, he mumbled, so much he'd wanted to be. He was afraid. I held his hand, waiting for some breath of reconciliation, deathbed peace.

"No time now," he said.

I watched him go down the stony path, the broad sway of his red robes swinging with each careful step. I'd expected something more from Lama: profound advice, instruction, something whispered. Instead, a light wind only, the stones, dust pressed deep inside my skin. "No time now," he said.

I couldn't quite admit I'd come all this way for noth-ing. Beads of perspiration bubbled down my neck, my arms, collected in the hollow of my chest. There were crickets, a small stream rippling, the indignant tramp of horses far ahead on the path. Wind at my back. White sun burning overhead.

Everyone, I thought, has his Tibet, his dream, his mountain cave: and this is mine. I had not thought the view would be so clear, nor so clearly ordinary. It's some-thing of a relief to leave it and follow after the others.

The stony path ends in a field of yellow grass beside a river. A nylon umbrella is set up to shade Lama from the sun. He spreads his *sham tab* on the ground beneath him for a carpet. Kagi makes a fire, collecting sticks, dried stalks of grass, pats of dung, then unstrings a sack containing kettles, tea, and food from a horse's saddle. I head down to the water, where the men who own the horses crouch, splashing each other, laughing, thin, clear streams raining from their hair.

Not far from the water's edge is a small mound of *mani* stones like the ones I saw in Yushu, with mantras chiseled on their faces. I wander over, standing awhile, tracing the sacred syllables whose meaning eludes me. I finger the small envelope in my pocket, which contains a whisker from a dead cat, a lock of Neff's hair, a few strands of my ex-lover's. Meant to be left inside the cave, but here will have to do. As an afterthought, I add a few hairs of my own, then slip the envelope between the stones. Surprising, how easy it is to bury the dead.

After lunch we climb back on our horses and ride toward Korche. It's slow going, uphill most of the way, through tangled walls of stunted shrub, fording rivers. If we pass a village, we have to stop for all the people who come running, limping, crawling out to honor Lama and gawk at the Americans perched gracelessly on restive horses. Silently, I swear that I'll remember their astonished smiles, their patched clothes, the mud caked on their hands and faces. I'll try to know them, in memory at least, the fevered play of half-formed images and fleeting words—bright fragments of an unseen whole. They are already what I'm becoming.

The sun is setting by the time we reach an area that feels somewhat familiar. I recognize the road, at any rate, if not the way to travel. With luck, we'll get to Korche before dark.

2 12/02